Simply
SoulStirring

Simply SoulStirring

WRITING AS A
MEDITATIVE PRACTICE

Francis Dorff, O. PRAEM.

PAULIST PRESS
New York   Mahwah, N. J.

Book design by Theresa M. Sparacio and Lynn Else

Jacket design by Cynthia Dunne

Copyright © 1998 by the Norbertine Community, Albuquerque, New Mexico

Library of Congress Cataloging-in-Publication Data

Dorff, Francis.
Simply soulstirring : writing as a meditative process / by Francis Dorff.
    p.   cm.
   "A Robert J. Wicks spirituality selection."
   Includes bibliographical references and index.
   ISBN 0-8091-0496-2 (cloth)
   1. Spiritual life –Catholic Church. 2. Spiritual journals –Authorship. 3. Meditation –Catholic Church. I. Title.
BX2350.2.D6465   1998
248.4´6–dc21   97-49222
                                                       CIP

Published by Paulist Press
997 Macarthur Boulevard
Mahwah, New Jersey 07430

Printed and bound in the
United States of America

CONTENTS

*This book is dedicated to
Ira Progoff,
mentor, colleague, and friend,
who has taught so many
how soul stirring writing can be.*

...to let the spiritual,
unbidden and unconscious,
grow up through the common;
this is my symphony.

—William Henry Channing

PROLOGUE:

SOULSTIRRING

When your soul stirs,
take attentive note.

"imply soulstirring!"

What a gift a soul-stirring experience is. It puts us in touch not just with our bodies, thoughts, or feelings but with the inner core of our whole being. It makes us aware, if only for a moment, that there is a depth and meaning to our lives that go beyond superficial appearances and personal possessions. It makes us aware that we have an inner life—that we are not one-dimensional islands but many-dimensional parts of the Main. If only for a moment, a soul-stirring experience lends a deeper-than-personal resonance and quality to our lives.

Soul stirrings are very special gifts. One leads to another, and as they accumulate, they begin to expand our life in two directions. At first they expand it inwardly, by extending the depth, range, capacity, and quality of our thoughts and feelings. In time, soul stirrings expand our life outwardly as well, by suggesting creative things for us to do and by lending a soulful quality to our actions and relationships. Our soulful awareness then begins to diffuse itself throughout our being, and we find ourselves living "magnanimous"—"big soul"—lives from the inside out.

Soul stirrings are important gifts not only for each of us but also for all of us. We live in a time in which many of us have lost our soul. By that I do not mean that we are going to hell, although it may feel like that at times. What I mean is that we have lost touch with the reality of our inner life. We live as though our life were limited to what we see, get, and have on the surface. We equate this one-dimensional life with *real living* and the *real world*. In this context, any reference to *soul-stirring* and an *inner world* seems strange and *unreal* to us, even though we may find it curiously intriguing. When we are out of touch with our own soul, we live as one-dimensional islands unaware of our own inner depth, wealth, mystery, and connection to the Main.

Soul stirrings are doubly important for all of us at this time since we are living in a time of unprecedented change. At such times, soul stirrings frequently carry an intimation of the next creative step to be taken in our lives, our communities, and our culture. If we are out of touch with our soul, however, we do not notice and cultivate these soul stirrings and are left with the dis-integrating reality of what we have.

Part of that disintegrating reality is reflected in the fact that the souls of many of us no longer seem to be stirred by the esthetic, political, philosophical, and religious symbols that have stirred the souls of other women and men for generations. These traditional symbols seem to have lost their power.

To compound the situation, we are bombarded by an unprecedented barrage of external stimuli that makes it increasingly difficult for us even to notice the much more subtle stirrings of our own soul. When we do notice our soul stirring, we often do not know what to make of it. So we tend to forget about it and get back to the *"real world."* In the process, we further distance ourselves from the reality and movement of our own inner lives.

The whole movement of modern psychology can be seen to be an ongoing attempt to address this contemporary loss of soul and to help us, as modern persons, reconnect with the reality of our own inner lives. Early in this century, Carl Jung wrote a book entitled *Modern Man in Search of a Soul,* which sounded the keynote for this soul-searching enterprise. Subsequent developments in psychology have documented and attempted to facilitate that quest. They have tried to put soul back in psychology itself and have developed such soulful psychologies as analytic, third force, fourth force, holistic, depth, transpersonal, and the *soul-making* psychologies of Hillman and Moore. In Thomas Moore's happy

2

terms, "the care of the soul" and the experience of "soul mates" are once again becoming urgent personal and cultural concerns.

For many of us, however, the personal question still remains: "How can I learn to become more aware of the stirrings of my own soul, and to nurture and cultivate them so that I may live a more soulful life?"

There are many practical ways to address this question. This book describes just one of them. It is a simple, traditional, classical, meditative way of noting, exploring, and following the stirrings of our soul: writing.

For over forty years now, I have been a member of the monastic tradition of the Order of Premontre, in which the practice of meditative writing is deeply rooted in the Judeo-Christian scriptures and in the lifelong example of our spiritual father, Augustine of Hippo. Over the past twenty years, I have also been working closely with depth psychologist Dr. Ira Progoff on his pioneering work of introducing persons to writing as a tool for personal and spiritual growth. My indebtedness to both of these traditions is interwoven throughout this book, as it is throughout my life.

I am also indebted to Dr. Robert Wicks, who not only suggested that I write the original article on which this book is based but also encouraged me to revise and expand it into a book. I am grateful to Joan Crone as well, who shared her beautiful home and her extensive library on diary and journal writing with me, and gave me a personally printed copy of the soul-stirring quotation of William Henry Channing with which this book begins. I also want to thank Margaia Forcier-Call, Joseph Schmidt, F.C.S., and Joseph Serano, O. Praem., for their helpful suggestions after reading this book in manuscript form. I am especially grateful to my editor, Maria Maggi, who worked with such care and enthusiasm to make this book a thing of beauty.

I probably do not even have to mention that this book is not meant to be a comprehensive treatment of meditative writing. It is meant only as a simple primer to tempt and encourage you to see if the simple act of writing can stir your soul and help you live more soulfully.

Nor does this book mean to imply that meditative writing is for everyone. There are many different ways to keep in touch with our soul and to cultivate its stirrings. Writing is merely one of them. If we are drawn to it, however, writing can be an extremely important way of working with our soul. The way to tell whether or not we are drawn to meditative writing is to try it. Basically, that is what this book is all about: to encourage you to try meditative writing.

With that in mind, we will describe first the *process*, then the general *character*, of meditative writing as they are reflected in a Zen story. Finally, we will describe several ways of *practicing* meditative writing that can help you get started in this work. By way of a fully conscious pun, two "Postscripts"—for there is no real substitute for the experience of writing itself—provide some historical background and an annotated list of readings, both of which may be helpful to those interested in further exploring the practice of meditative writing. Finally, the footnotes are gathered together as leads for further practice in meditative writing.

In the workshops and retreats that I give in meditative writing, I sometimes have the feeling that I am sitting on a bridge greeting people as they cross over from one side to the other. It is a narrow footbridge, and the people cross it one by one, going in two different directions. They cross it by writing.

One group is made up of deeply spiritual persons who have so equated their soul with their religion that they have begun to disregard its stirrings in their everyday lives. I love to greet them as they cross the bridge of meditative writing to discover their souls stirring in their lives as a whole.

The other group is made up of persons who, because they are not formally religious, have come to think that there is no spiritual dimension to their lives. I love to greet them too, as they cross the bridge of meditative writing to discover how soulful their lives actually are.

The bridge of meditative writing has a way of reconnecting us with aspects of our lives from which we have become divorced. It also has a way of uniting us with persons from whom we think we are divided. Meditative writing is an integrating bridge. It is a bridge of inner meeting, or a bridge of soul-stirring communion.

As I complete this book, I feel as though I am sitting on the bridge of meditative writing once again. I regret that this time I will not be able to greet the people who may be crossing it to discover the stirrings of their own souls, and to cultivate lives of soulful connection. May our souls greet in those stirrings, however. May it be so.

Thanksgiving, 1996
Norbertine Center for the Spiritual Life
Albuquerque, New Mexico

The Process of Meditative Writing

"The First Principle"

 hen one goes to Obaku Temple in Kyoto one sees carved over the gate the words "The First Principle."

The letters are unusually large, and those who appreciate calligraphy always admire them as being a masterpiece. They were drawn by Kosen two hundred years ago.

When the master drew them he did so on paper, from which workmen made the larger carving in wood. As Kosen sketched the letters a bold pupil was with him who had made several gallons of ink for the calligraphy and who never failed to criticize his master's work.

"That is not good," he told Kosen after the first effort.

"How is that one?"

"Poor. Worse than before," pronounced the pupil.

Kosen patiently wrote one sheet after another until eighty-four First Principles had accumulated, still without the approval of the pupil.

Then, when the young man stepped outside for a few moments, Kosen thought: "Now is my chance to escape his keen eye," and he wrote hurriedly, with a mind free from distraction: "The First Principle."

"A masterpiece," pronounced the pupil.*

Even though it is speaking about calligraphy, this story has a lot to tell us about the art of meditative writing as a whole. It starts out by telling about what people, for centuries, have considered to be a classic piece of soul-stirring writing. The story does not focus on *what* was written, however; it focuses instead on *how* it was written. From this point on, what becomes impor-

---

*Reps, Paul (ed.), *Zen Flesh, Zen Bones* (New York: Doubleday, n.d.), p. 23.

tant in the story is not so much the beautiful *product* that the master creates but the meditative *process* through which he becomes creative. It is this soul-stirring *process*, above all, that we want to note in what follows.

Practicing Patiently

After focusing on *how* the master writes, the story of "The First Principle" then goes on to describe the general movement of the master's meditative process.

First of all, he practices humbly, diligently, and patiently. In the beginning, he does so under the "keen eye" of his critical pupil with what appears to be diminishing returns. The harder he tries to please his critical pupil, the more self-conscious he seems to become and the less spontaneous his writing is. Eighty-four *failures* accumulate. Undaunted, the master continues to practice, beginning afresh each time, simply doing the best he can.

When the pupil "steps outside for a few moments," the master is ready to seize the uncluttered moment. Without concern for the pupil's "keen eye" and without even time to think about what he is doing, the master writes hurriedly, "with a mind free from distraction." He is now writing from the private, unself-conscious, meditative place from which masterpieces come.

When the critical pupil returns, he gives his enthusiastic approval to the outcome. "A masterpiece," he declares.

While the master no doubt graciously accepts his pupil's compliment, he probably does not need to be told about the quality of his work. He knows his work from the inside out. He knows intuitively that what he has written is of a piece with the process, the inner place, and the person from whom it has come. He knows better than anyone the capacity his writing may have to stir others' souls—it has stirred his own soul, first of all.

Honoring the "Bold Pupil"

hen we first hear the story of "The First Principle," we tend to take the figure of the bold pupil literally. We think of him as an impudent, arrogant youngster who has the audacity to criticize the master's work. We wonder why he does not just stick to making ink and why the master allows himself to be criticized by such an upstart.

There is another way to look at the bold pupil, however. We can look at him as a symbol of the "bold pupil" who is within the master himself. We can look at the bold pupil as a figure of the master's own self-conscious mind, which wants to criticize, control, and take credit for everything the master does.

When we think of the bold pupil in this symbolic way, we begin to see that the master has at least three ways in which he can handle his pupil.

The *first pathway* the master could take would be simply to tell the bold pupil off. He could ask him who he thinks he is, remind him who is master here, humiliate him, and put him in his place. Of course, in doing so, the master would have to become triumphantly self-conscious himself, and perhaps even somewhat angry and arrogant. For some of us, this may appear to be the only reasonable course of action for the master to take. The master, however, does not take it.

The *second pathway* the master could take would be to ignore the bold pupil. He could simply disregard whatever the bold pupil has to say and just go about his writing. In this passive way, the master would be sending the pupil a very clear message: "Get off my back. What you have to say is of no consequence." The master does not take this pathway either.

Instead, the master takes the *third pathway*. He himself becomes a pupil again and listens attentively to whatever his critic says. By listening to his critic in this way, he discovers not only how far the bold pupil's comments can take him, but also that they cannot take him nearly far enough.

Paradoxically, by listening attentively to the bold pupil, the master eventually silences him. Having been listened to with such docility, the bold pupil seems to run out of things to say. He now feels free to take a break. In this break, the master writes in a way he was unable to write while the bold pupil was present and presiding. He writes in a free-flowing, spontaneous way, "with a mind free from distraction." In other words, he writes from his soul, masterfully.

When we read the story in this way, the bold pupil's gifts and limitations become clear to us, as well. On the one hand, he can prepare the ink but he cannot do the soul-stirring writing. His "keen eye" and his outspokenness allow him to criticize his master's writing, to help his master hone the discipline of his craft, and to recognize a masterpiece when he sees one. On the other hand, the bold pupil's keen eye and critical spirit keep him from being able personally to enter the soulful space from which masterpieces come. As long as that is the case, the bold pupil remains merely a critic, a commentator, and an apprentice, not a master himself.

The return of the bold pupil, however, is well worth noting, since it puts him in a very different relationship with the master than he was at the outset of the story. Prior to his "stepping outside for a few moments," the bold pupil's critical comments could have deterred the master from writing from the soulful place within himself. On the other side of the master's having written "with a mind free from distraction," however, the bold pupil returns to put his "keen eye," his enthusiasm, and all of his critical intelligence in service of the master's soul. "A masterpiece," he exclaims. He has now found his proper place as a servant and a student, not a master of the soul. It is in this capacity that the master can now collaborate most soulfully with him.

Embodying "The First Principle"

hen we first hear the story of "The First Principle," we may think that it tells us nothing of what the First Principle of Zen actually is. All it appears to tell us is that Master Kosen wrote "The First Principle" that now marks the gateway to the Temple.

In thinking this way, we may believe that the story focuses only on *what* the master has written. If we recognize that it focuses primarily on *how* the master is writing, however, we begin to realize that the story is telling us much more about the First Principle than we may have thought. It is telling us that the First Principle of Zen is hidden within the master's action—within *how* he writes.

The master writes with a beginner's mind, patiently practicing his writing until it empties his mind and becomes the gateway to the place where he and his writing are one. He writes with the openness of a learner's mind, so that, in the act of writing itself, pupil, master, and meditating become one. The practice of writing is clearly the master's own portal to the Temple. It is his pathway to the self-forgetful attentiveness to all of life that is at the heart of Zen. In other words, the practice of writing is one of the ways in which the master not only writes "The First Principle," but personally embodies it.

Working Privately

t the heart of it all, the story of "The First Principle" presents the master's meditative writing as a very private work. It takes place while the bold pupil is away, and long before the wood-carvers arrive. When his writing becomes most creative, the master is all alone—in more ways than one.

The "bold pupil" has left him. So has: his concern for pleasing his pupil; his concern for doing a good job with this important commission; his thoughts about how his work might be admired by others as they enter the Temple in times to come; his memory of his eighty-four previous attempts; and perhaps even his personal misgivings about whether he is capable of writing soulfully anymore.

The master no longer has time for all of this outer and inner company. He writes "hurriedly, with a mind free from distraction." For the moment, he is totally immersed in writing. He is all alone. His writing does not come from the admonitions of his bold pupil. It does not come from his carefully analyzing what went wrong with his eighty-four other attempts. It seems to come from nothing, from nowhere, from no one. It comes spontaneously from within the master, as though it were his very first attempt. In a sense, it is. The master is writing with a beginner's mind. He is so totally attentive to his writing that he and his writing are one. Writing in this way is a very private—a very meditative—work.

Following the Meditative Movement

hen we begin to appreciate the intimately private nature of the heart of meditative writing, we are inclined to equate it with meditative writing as a whole. After all, it is the heart of the process, is it not?

It is important to note that while the story of "The First Principle" does present the master's private, unself-conscious writing as the heart of the process of meditative writing, it does not equate that moment with the whole process of meditative writing itself.

Actually, the story describes the meditative writing of the master as a three-step movement. First of all, there is the *patient practice* through which the master writes his way through distractions to the quiet, solitary place within himself. Then, there is the unself-conscious writing "with a mind free from distraction" that the master does from within this private, soulful place. Finally, there is not only the approval of the bold pupil as the master completes his work but also, as we can well imagine, the master's careful supervision of the wood-carvers' work so that it will be true to his original inspiration. This careful supervision allows his writing to take the public form that inspires the admiration of centuries of pilgrims whose souls are stirred by seeing it.

From this perspective, the meditative writing of the master is not just about his being able to write from a very private, soulful place within himself. It is about his practicing a process through which he continually allows his writing to lead him inward, to keep him inward, and to lead him outward again.

In practicing this process through his meditative writing, the master is mirroring the way in which life itself meditates. Life meditates by spontaneously moving us inward from the active concerns of the day, through the gradual quieting of our bodies and minds, to the private place of dreaming, and then outward again to the active concerns of another day.

In this instance, life's meditative movement is not just about experiencing dreams. It is about knitting together our daytime and nighttime awareness; the conscious and the unconscious dimensions of our lives; the personal and the more-than-personal levels of our experience; our inspirations and enterprises; our inner and outer worlds; the spontaneous and the studied dimensions of our lives.

In a much longer cycle, life also meditates by spontaneously moving us from times of relative stability, through the soul-stirring cycle of disintegration, to times of new integration. In this instance as well, life's natural meditative movement is not just about revealing the naked depths of our being; it is about knitting together the many dimensions of our lives in a most creative way.

The same is true of the movement of the master's meditative writing. It is not just about writing spontaneously from a private, inner place. It is about writing as a way of knitting together the many dimensions of his life.

Through his meditative writing, the master is following not only the movement through which life naturally meditates, but also the movement that flows through most of the classical meditative practices. Although these practices take myriad forms, they seem to share a common meditative movement through which we can cultivate our life's integrating rhythm of moving inward from its surface to its depths, staying inward either actively or passively for a while, and moving outward again from the depths of our life to its surface. This is the integrating movement that not only stirs our souls but also helps us to cultivate soulful lives.

If we think of meditation apart from this integrating movement, we often equate it with staying inward. The master's writing, most meditative practices, and life itself try to teach us that meditating involves us in much more than just staying inward. It involves us in following an ongoing, soul-stirring cycle of moving inward, staying inward, and moving outward again.

Had the master lacked the patience to make eighty-four well-observed first attempts, he may never have found his way to the private, soulful place within himself, or have developed the well-honed skills to give appropriate form to what he experienced in that place. Had he equated meditative writing with just staying inward, "The First Principle" would not be stirring the souls of pilgrims and inviting them not just to enter the Obaku Temple, but to enter the Temple within themselves so that they too might live soulfully. For, as the master continues to follow life's meditative movement through his writing, this is what the quality of his work and life eventually become: an increasingly eloquent witness and invitation to writing and living soulfully.

Living Soulfully

any of us are inclined to think of writing as one thing, meditating as another, and living as still something else. While in a sense this can be true, we have seen something very different happening as the master practices meditative writing. We have seen how the master's writing, meditating, and living tend to become one.

This is how it is with any meditative practice that we allow to run its full course. It begins to cultivate a soulful, unifying quality of movement and awareness in us that tends, quite naturally, to overflow into our lives as a whole. In admiring the text of "The First Principle" as a masterpiece, the bold pupil and the visitors to the Temple are also admiring the underlying unity of the master's life.

Whether others sense this underlying unity or not, the master definitely embodies it. He embodies it in his patient practice; in the way in which he honors the bold pupil, in his writing with a beginner's mind, in his finding a soulful place within himself beyond the distracted mind, where his writing, meditating, and living are one; and in his following the meditative movement that allows him, however inadequately, to express publicly the depths of his soul through the quality of his writing and living.

Practicing the SoulStirring Process

he master's example brings us back to where we started in our reflections on the story of "The First Principle." It brings us back to the important fact that the primary focus of the story is not on the beautiful *product* that the master creates, but on the soul-stirring *process* through which he becomes creative.

If we think that the master's writing is merely about creating a beautiful *product,* then we probably picture him retiring after he has written "The First Principle" for the gateway to the Temple of Obaku. After all, he has achieved his goal, hasn't he? He has created a masterpiece. Even the bold pupil said so.

If what the master's writing is really about, however, is practicing a soul-stirring *process* through which his writing, meditating, and living can continually become one, then we can easily picture him sitting at his desk the very next day, patiently practicing with a beginner's mind under the keen eye of his bold pupil, and perhaps generating yet another spate of first drafts. From time to time, the master's writing may generate a masterful *product,* but what he is really about, day in and day out, is practicing a soul-stirring *process* through which his whole life becomes meditative, creative, and soulful.

❧

The Character
of Meditative
Writing

❧

Writing as a Practice

y giving us the example of a master for whom writing is clearly a way of getting in touch with his soul and living soulfully, the story of "The First Principle" can help us find out whether or not writing can become a way of meditating and of living meditatively for us as well. It can only do this, however, if we allow it to convince us that writing is writing. Writing is not talking about writing. It is not thinking about writing. It is not reading about writing. It is not preparing to write. Writing is writing.

The only way in which we can actually find out if writing can stir our soul and help us live more soulfully is to write. If, in one word, we want to know what writing is all about, the answer is *writing*. If we would like a more elaborate answer than that, the answer is, "Writing, writing, writing."

In this regard, the story of "The First Principle" can be a great help to us. In its simplicity, it cuts through all of the customary substitutes for actually writing that our cluttered minds and our own "bold pupil" often impose on us.

The mere suggestion of writing frightens some of us. We *know* we are not writers. Some of our early teachers may have made that very clear to us. Consequently, before we start writing, we think we have to take a course in writing, or read an armful of books on writing, or read *what* the best writers have written, or go shopping for the best writing implements and materials.

We may even do all of this preparatory work on the assumption that, when we finally do get around to writing, our first effort will be admired by everyone as "a masterpiece." In that case, it might help us to remember the Master Kosen's initial eighty-four drafts of The First Principle. It might also be helpful to note that, when we are thinking in this way, what we actually have in mind is not our soul but our reputation.

More often than not, our remote preparations for writing become so engrossing, so distracting, or so discouraging that we never really do get around to doing much writing and finding out whether or not writing is a congenial meditative practice for us.

If we add the adjectives *meditative* or *soul-stirring* to writing as we are doing here, the prospect of writing becomes even more intimidating for many of us. Even if we enjoy writing, we may *think* that our writing has nothing to do with meditation or our soul. We may *think* that we are extroverts—and not particularly religious or spiritual ones at that.

In addition, we may equate meditative or soulful writing with writing about "holy" or "religious" things—things in which we may have little interest and about which we may think we know little or nothing.

In that case, we may begin to think that, in order to do meditative writing, we will really have to bone up on spirituality by reading a lot more about religion, meditation, and transpersonal psychology. For many of us, this is such a daunting prospect in itself that, in all probability, we either give it up before long or get lost in it. In either case, we never will find out whether writing can actually be for us a soul-stirring way of meditating and of living meditatively.

If, on the other hand, we are quite familiar with meditation, but equate meditating with the practice of sitting quietly, staying inward, and trying to think, feel, and do nothing, then we have yet another seemingly insurmountable problem. Meditative writing will then strike us as a contradiction in terms, right from the start. To our mind, meditating and writing are mutually exclusive. We either meditate or we write; we cannot do both at the same time.

The story of "The First Principle" is most helpful in this regard. With disarming simplicity, it cuts through all of our clear and perhaps rigid concepts about writing and meditating. It simply suggests that, if we really want to discover whether or not writing can become a meditative practice for us, we do what the master does, namely write. It suggests that the practice of writing itself will teach us all we really have to know about meditative writing and the unique way in which each of us is to go about it.

This suggestion is so simple that it comes almost as an insult to our sophisticated, "bold pupil" minds. If we take this suggestion to heart, however, and just start writing, after a while, we will know beyond a doubt whether or not writing is a way of growing and living soulfully for us.

This action-oriented approach to writing can be a very important spiritual lesson for us. It can teach us that we learn and grow spiritually by doing—by practicing. It can teach us that writing is a practice, not in the sense of preparing to do something more important, but in the very same sense in which meditating is a practice. It is a work in which we regularly engage ourselves, regardless of the outcome. It is a work that we value for its own sake. It is a work that reveals its undeniable value to us as we practice it.

Writing as a Private Practice

e often begin devoting ourselves to the practice of writing with the thought of writing something for others to read. This is a good place to start. The problem is, many of us tend to stop there. As we continue the practice of writing, however, we begin writing things that we realize are nobody's business but our own. Little by little, our writing begins to teach us that, deep down, it is an intimately private practice. It begins to show us the qualitative difference between writing for someone else and writing for ourselves alone.

By initiating us into its radically private character in this way, our writing gives us another important spiritual lesson. It challenges the assumption of an extroverted, sensate, one-dimensional culture that maintains that what you see is all there is, and that everyone has a right to see all there is of us. It helps us cultivate a private life and introduces us to the reality of our own inner world, and to the inalienable solitude of our soul.

Once we begin to experience the difference between public and private writing in this way, our private, meditative writing begins to become the cutting edge of our writing practice. It teaches us how to write for ourselves alone, without intending to impress, edify, amuse, or enlighten someone else. As it does so, our writing gradually weans us away from the comparisons, evaluations, judgments, and innumerable shoulds and oughts that frequently come from writing with someone else in mind. It is as though our private writing invites not only our own "bold pupil" but also anyone else we may have in mind, to "step outside for a moment" and to leave us alone to write "with a mind free from distraction."

At first, the experience of solitude involved in this kind of intimately private writing can be very frightening to us. We can invent a thousand different ways in which to avoid it, such as dusting our desk again, rewriting what we have already written, making urgent telephone calls, taking a nap, or reading what someone else who "really knows how to write" has written.

If, instead of fleeing from this solitude, we can learn to enter it and write from within it, we can begin to experience what it actually means to become one with our writing and to write "with a mind free from distraction." Then we no longer have to screen, judge, or edit our writing for the approval of others. We can simply let it flow so that it can honestly mirror to us the stirrings of our own soul.

As our private writing begins to flow in this way, it tends to become increasingly personal, honest, and revelatory. It tends to become the most honest reflection there may be of who we really are and of what we really are about. It begins to reflect not only a me nobody knows but also a me whom we ourselves may not know all that well. Little by little, our writing begins to introduce us to our own soul—our whole inner world. As it does so, it often takes on a meditative, soul-stirring quality that surprises us, and that sometimes contrasts starkly with the atmosphere closer to the surface of our lives.

When our meditative writing begins to move, and to move us in this way, it often feels as though it is coming from some inner sanctuary. This may puzzle or embarrass us, at first, but eventually, we simply have to admit that that is how it is. We have to admit that, at times, our writing has a way of taking us to a meditative place and coming directly from this deep, uncensored place within ourselves. Free to become whatever it wants to become, our private writing now begins to become a mirror of our soul, and of how our soul spontaneously moves toward what it most deeply desires. Our writing becomes soul-stirring.

While much of the content of this kind of writing tends to remain private, just as our soul itself remains private, its meditative quality and movement tend to overflow into our life as a whole, and to become a wellspring for a much more personal, creative, and soulful way of relating, communicating, and living than we may ever have known before.

Writing as a Meditative Practice

e may begin writing with a very clear idea of what meditation is. For us, meditation may be saying our prayers, or talking to God, or sitting in silence, or allowing a prayer phrase to quiet our minds, or reflecting on a treasured text from Sacred Writings, or walking reflectively, or thinking religious thoughts, or immersing ourselves in sentiments of love, praise, and thanksgiving, or some other classical form of praying with which we are familiar.

All of these can be effective *forms* of meditation, but meditating is not just a *form*. It is a soul-stirring *process* that runs through all of these forms. As we have seen, meditating is a soul-stirring process of going inward, staying inward to experience and explore the reality of our inner world, and coming outward to act and live soulfully. If we are practicing one of these other forms of meditating, then, it may seem to us that to begin the practice of writing would just give us one more thing to do.

In this context, I think of a woman who had come to equate meditation with Zen sitting. This form of meditation had become an important part of her life. At the same time, she was feeling strongly drawn to write, which she thought was something very different from meditating.

One day, her Zen teacher approached her and asked, "Why are you sitting in meditation when writing is your way of meditating?"

On one level, the woman was surprised by what her teacher said. On another level, she was greatly relieved by it. It affirmed what she had already begun to suspect but was afraid to admit. From then on, writing officially became for her what it had already unofficially begun to be: her primary soul-stirring practice.

This woman was fortunate in having an open-minded meditation teacher. We do not have to have a meditation teacher, however, to discover whether or not writing can become a soul-stirring practice for us. Writing itself can be the best teacher of all. If writing is a meditative way for us, before long it will take us to soulful inner places in which we can be alone, be ourselves, and begin honestly experiencing and exploring the many dimensions of our lives and how these many dimensions are interconnected with one another and with life as a whole. In time, our private writing will probably begin to generate thoughts and inspirations that want to be expressed in a more public way. It will also begin to generate a soulful attitude and atmosphere that will want to permeate our lives as a whole.

When we find ourselves being caught up in this soul-stirring movement of meditative writing, we begin to recognize that writing is beginning to do the same thing that any of our other meditative practices may have been doing. It is beginning to knit together the many dimensions of our lives with soulful integrity by leading us inward, helping us to stay within ourselves for a while, and leading us outward again. We then know, not by hearsay but by our personal experience, that writing can be a soul-stirring practice, just like any of the other classical ways of meditating.

We may also begin to discover that any of the other *forms* of meditation that we may be practicing can be greatly enhanced and complemented by describing and exploring in writing what we are experiencing as we dedicate ourselves to these meditative practices. As we make this discovery, writing begins to take its rightful place as a meditative practice in itself.

Writing as a Creative Practice

hen we first begin meditative writing, we often approach it as a way of recording what we already know. We write down things so that we will not forget them or so that we may share them with others just as a ship's captain records the events of the day in the ship's log.

While this is a natural place to start, meditative writing can teach us much more than this. Otherwise, it would just be a way of taking notes on the comments of our bold pupil and reinforcing our conscious attitudes about what we already know.

As we continue to practice writing, we sometimes find ourselves doing so "with a mind free from distraction." At such times, our writing gradually moves us into deeper, more intimately personal, wholly uncharted waters, taking us beyond the security of what we already know to let us discover what we did not know we knew. Then we discover just how creative writing can be. Sometimes, we discover this while we are in the very process of writing. At other times, it is only as we read back to ourselves what we have written that we discover how creative our writing actually is.

As our meditative writing starts to become creative, our first reaction to our discoveries is often surprise. "Where did that come from?" we often catch ourselves saying. "Soul-stirring!" would be another appropriate reaction, since that is what is actually going on. Our meditative writing is beginning to reverse what we thought and to reveal what we did not expect. It is becoming a most creative meditative channel for discovering the inner and outer facts of our own lives.

This description may strike some of us as farfetched. It may sound like something that might happen once in a lifetime to some guru or mystic in some distant land, but certainly not to us.

(If we listen closely to the accent in this kind of thinking, however, we may be struck by how much it sounds like the voice of our own "bold critic.")

As our writing begins to become a channel of deeper-than-conscious knowing for us, however, its creative character becomes not a claim to fame but a simple matter of fact. We know first-hand how the simple practice of writing has the capacity to surprise, challenge, threaten, illuminate, and draw us beyond our conscious and habitual ways of experiencing and understanding. We know that writing can reveal to us what we did not know we knew. It can reveal to us the wisdom of our soul. Even if no one else ever sees it, such writing is creative writing in the most personal and profound sense of that word.

I am reminded of an elderly woman who sat with her eyes closed through most of a journal-writing workshop that I was giving. There she was with a peaceful smile lighting up her face and a full journal unopened on her lap. She stayed that way, despite my most eloquent invitations to the participants to do the writing exercises I was describing.

Eventually, she approached me and said, "Young man, I just want you to know that I am not writing because my life has told me all that it has to tell me. But I enjoy being in the atmosphere created by people working in their own lives. So, if you don't mind, I will just sit here and enjoy it."

"That's fine," I replied, "but sometimes people who have lived and written as much as you have like to flip open their journal at any spot and read whatever they have written there."

"Thank you for that suggestion," she said with a gleam in her eye. "I may just give that a try."

When I looked back a while later, there she was, bent over her journal, writing. She *thought* that her life had no more to tell her. As she read back what she had written before, however, she *experienced* her soul stirring and began to write beyond what she had thought.

Another example of the creative character of meditative writing immediately comes to mind. We were about to begin a writing exercise in a journal workshop when a woman protested that she could not do it because she had been diagnosed as having writer's block. The leader quietly suggested that she write this in her journal and encouraged us to proceed with the exercise.

When we had finished the exercise and were given the opportunity to read, the woman read for about ten minutes.

"Are you the one with the writing block?" the leader asked.

"Yes," the woman answered.

"Oh," he replied. "Would anyone else like to read?"

The leader could have spent a long time analyzing or trying to talk the woman out of her writer's block. Had he done that, however, we would not have been writing. We might still be there, too, and the woman's "writing block" would probably be even better documented, lamented, and reinforced than it had been in the first place.

Instead, we invited the woman to trust the creative power of writing. With that, she wrote her way right through her writer's block. Her writing had become creative. It had created a completely new personal situation in her life.

Were we to multiply examples of this kind, the point of them all would be the same. It would be to encourage us to start writing to see whether or not writing becomes a private, soul-stirring, creative practice for us as well. In the next section, we will do that in yet another way, by suggesting some practical ways to begin practicing meditative writing.

Practicing
Meditative
Writing

Some Hints for Getting Started

hen we approach writing as a meditative exercise, many of the hints that help people get started in meditating become helpful in getting us started in writing as well. Three such hints involve place, time, and tools.

The Place

In most kinds of meditating, it is helpful to have an uncluttered place set apart especially for our meditative practice. The same is true for meditative writing. It can be a corner of our bedroom, our desk, a place on the porch, the kitchen table when it is not otherwise in use, a chapel, a corner of a garden, or some other place that we dedicate at certain times to our personal work of soul stirring. If we look for such a place, we will find it.

In time, that place begins to carry the atmosphere of the meditative writing we do there. It becomes a symbol of our dedication to the work of maintaining and cultivating our relationship with our own soul. Just going there can sometimes help us focus on the meditative work at hand, "with a mind free from distraction."

Of course, our meditative writing, like our meditative life itself, refuses to be confined to any one place. It wants to become a movable feast, to be taken on the road so that we can do it almost anywhere. At the outset, and for our ongoing intensive inner work, however, it is still helpful to have a designated place for meditative writing.

The Time

Like any other meditative practice, writing takes time. It takes time not just for the writing itself but also for the germinating, ruminating, and just plain wasting time that is an integral part of such writing. Like any other meditative practice, our practice of writing is often enhanced, at the outset, by being done with some intensity on a regular basis. One or two random attempts do not make a practice. Nor are they enough to reveal the soul-stirring potential that meditative writing might have for us.

Morning, evening, and night are classic times for meditating. They can be congenial times for meditative writing as well. In time, the nature of the writing we are doing will show us when it wants to be done. The middle of the night and the early morning often turn out to be the best times for writing down our dream experiences. Morning is a natural time for the kind of meditative writing that anticipates or sets the tone for the day, while evening is a natural time for the kind of meditative writing that looks back over the experiences of the day in order to savor and learn from them.

Some of us will find that our rhythm for writing is more on a weekly than a daily basis. We will find certain days of the week more congenial than others for devoting time to meditative writing. Others will look forward to the more leisurely time of vacation or retreat in which to complement and intensify their regular practice of meditative writing, and to deepen and extend its scope.

While we may have to experiment in order to find the best time for our meditative writing, we need not experiment with writing down the day, month, year, and place, on every entry we make. We can take that as a rule well established by the experience of others. With them, we will find that the time and place of our original entry can be very important when, at a later date, we read what we have written.

If we look for a congenial time for doing our meditative writing, we will find it. In the process, we will probably discover something very important about the rhythm of our lives.

We do not have to go into debt to begin meditative writing. The tools are very simple, inexpensive, and available to everyone. Basically, they are the same tools that scribes have used for centuries: paper, ink, and pen, or for those of us who prefer its particular look, feel, and sound, a pencil. Even these simple tools lend themselves to some hints for beginning meditative writing.

It is helpful to have one notebook in which we do all of our soul-stirring work. The reason for this is that, in our meditative writing, we do not limit our work just to the religious or spiritual aspect of our experience. We allow it to extend to our experience of life as a whole. Using one notebook gives us one place in which to do the life-integrating work that our meditative writing can eventually become.

I think of a man who used to keep personal notes on his life on little scraps of paper that were all over the place. As he described it to me, his life was all over the place as well. I suggested that he tape his notes into a notebook, just as though it were a scrapbook of his life, and that he begin doing his life integrating work or meditative writing in that one scrapbook. In time, his life began coming together again, and his notebook reflected it.

Some people find it most helpful to use for their primary workbook a three-ring binder or a notebook with dividers. That format allows them to combine coherence with flexibility in their meditative writing. Others supplement their primary workbook with a small notebook that they carry in their pocket, so that they can briefly jot down experiences while they are still fresh. They later tape these jottings into their primary workbook and enlarge on them if they feel so inclined. The important thing in these notebook hints, however, is that we use one primary notebook for doing what eventually can become the life-integrating work of our meditative writing.

Of course, our meditative writing, like our lives, refuses to be limited to one notebook. In time, it will require that we keep a notebook for our current private work and store the notebooks that we have completed, for occasional reference. In addition, our private, meditative writing will most probably give rise to projects that want to be made public, such as letters, talks, articles, books, public or family journals, or other such creative projects. It is still important, however, that we not confuse our private, soul-stirring writing, which is the laboratory from which these public projects emerge, with these projects themselves, and that we dedicate one notebook especially to that private work.

In addition to pen or pencil, some people find it helpful to include colored pens or crayons among their writing tools, so that they can highlight entries, color-code them, illuminate certain words, or include colored doodlings and drawings as part of their meditative writing.

Among other possible writing tools are the typewriter and the computer. These can have certain advantages for those who are quite comfortable in using them. The typewriter and the computer lend themselves to enlarging on handwritten entries and making extensive entries in greater detail and in shorter time than writing by hand allows.

The down side of using a typewriter or a computer is that, for many of us, it tends to make our meditative writing much more verbose and heady. In addition, the typewriter and computer introduce both a mechanical element and a noise factor into our meditative work that, for some people, prove to be a drawback. The typewriter and the computer also lack the flexibility of handwriting, and fail to reflect our different moods, as the character of our handwriting often does so well.

For these reasons, if we are comfortable with using the typewriter and the computer, it is often more helpful in our soul-stirring work to use them as a complement to, rather than a substitute for, writing by hand.

Expanding Our Practice

hen we are introduced to meditative practice, we are often given a sampling of different approaches in order to expand our practice and allow us to discover what works for us. The following practical suggestions can help us get started in meditative writing and give us an initial feel for its character, scope, and life-integrating potential. We can then complement and expand these ways of working through our personal experimentation and the various additional writing exercises presented in many of the books listed in our Postscript on helpful reading.*

Those who want an approach to writing as a life-integrating discipline that is more comprehensive, integrated, and systematic than the following suggestions provide would do well to look into the Intensive Journal® method of Ira Progoff, as presented in his Dialogue House workshops and described in his book, *At a Journal Workshop.*

---

*Notable among these are Kathleen Adams's *The Way of the Journal;* Christina Baldwin's *One to One;* Harry J. Cargas's *Keeping a Spiritual Journal;* Sam Keen and Anne Valley-Fox's *Your Mythic Journey;* Morton T. Kelsey's *Adventure Inward;* Ronald Klug's *How to Keep a Spiritual Journal;* Tristine Rainer's *The New Diary,* and Richard Solly and Roseann Lloyd's *Journey Notes.*

Meditating

f we already have a meditative practice or a way of praying, that would be a good place to begin our meditative writing. Regardless of what form our customary meditative practice takes, we can begin by dating a new page in our notebook, becoming quiet, and describing in writing what goes on during our meditation. We can do this either during our meditative practice itself, if that is possible and comfortable for us, or immediately afterward. In either case, writing then becomes an integral part of our meditative practice.

Since, in meditative writing, we are writing only for our own eyes, we need not write in full sentences or polished prose. We can write in whatever way feels most natural and spontaneous to us and most honestly reflects our meditative work. I think of one woman who often wrote in circles, spinning her journal around like a potter's wheel.

Since, in meditative writing, we also want to be writing with the open mind of a beginner, we do not judge, screen, or edit anything that comes to us as we write. We simply accept it and record it as it is. We honestly describe not only the progress of our meditative work, therefore, but also what we consider to be its failures and distractions, as well as anything else that may come to us as we do so. It is important to note that, while we may judge some things to be distractions in the meditative work we are doing, there are no distractions in the meditative writing by which we describe it. We simply describe whatever goes on, without judging or classifying it. For some of us, that can be a great relief. It can also allow our meditative writing to become not only a complement to our other meditative work, but also a distinct meditative way of enhancing, enlarging, and relating it to our lives as a whole.

If we continue doing this kind of meditative writing, before long we will have much more than a written record of our meditative practice. We will have a much keener awareness of our inner life and how it relates to our life as a whole. We will also have tracings of the subtle thoughts, feelings, inspirations, soul stirrings, and inner movements that we would probably have overlooked or forgotten, had we not noted them immediately. In addition, we will know from our own experience how writing can be a meditative experience in its own right.

Becoming Quiet

ne of the first movements involved in most of the classical ways of meditating is to allow ourselves to become quiet. This is an important part of the initial meditative movement of going inward, as well as of the whole soulful atmosphere that begins to establish itself through meditative practice.

Frequently, as soon as we become quiet, we are bombarded by thoughts, feelings, memories, and projects that we feel we should be doing, all of which we consider to be distractions. Many of us then spend most, if not all, of our meditative time fighting against these distractions.

Since the mind of a beginner does not distinguish between what is meditative material and what are just distractions, writing with a beginner's mind can be a very helpful way of becoming quiet. As we honor whatever comes to us simply by writing it down as honestly as we can, we find that most of these experiences do not want to be pursued. They are like little children who just want to get our attention for a moment and then run away. They are like Master Kosen's "bold pupil" who, once his presence is honored, feels free to take a break.

In order to try this way of writing meditatively, we simply write the date on a new page in our notebook, become quiet, and for about ten minutes or so, briefly record whatever comes to us from our quietness.

Perhaps to our surprise, we may begin to discover that writing is a way both of noticing our experiences *and* of letting them disappear. As they disappear, the mind is emptied of its surface concerns and becomes even more quiet. From the other side of this quietness, more subtle inner experiences, of a qualitatively different kind, often begin to emerge. We are then free to honor them by writing them down. Afterward, we gradually come away from our meditative writing, read back to ourselves what we have written, and make any additional entries that come to us.

Though it can reveal much more, this exercise in meditative writing can let us experience how merely taking written inventory of our inner and outer experiences can be a way of actively becoming quiet.

Taking Texts to Heart

any of the classical ways of meditating help us take an important text or piece of Sacred Writing to heart in order to savor its deeper meaning and allow it to become part of our life. In the Christian monastic tradition this practice is called *lectio divina,* or "divine reading." It is a way of reading not just for information but for personal transformation. It is a way of reading in order to be *stirred up*—thoughtfully, emotionally, and spiritually.

When we do this kind of meditative reading we read a text with inner attentiveness until we feel our soul stir. It is like reading a treasured text in braille, only with the fingers of our heart. When we feel our soul stir, we discontinue reading and begin attending to these soul stirrings, enkindling them as we would sparks caught in tinder.

If we are already accustomed to meditating in this way, a place to begin meditative writing is by carefully writing out the text on which we will be meditating.

If we are not accustomed to this kind of meditative reading, a helpful exercise might be to date a fresh page in our notebook, become quiet, and make a list of texts that are or have been personally important to us. We need not limit our list to texts that religious traditions consider to be sacred. We can include poems or passages from other kinds of writing that have touched us, including personal letters.

When we make such a list of treasured texts, we are often surprised by the number and character of the texts that surface and with the memories and associations that frequently come along with them. Just the list can stir our souls. We can then choose one text from our list and begin to transcribe it as an exercise in meditative writing.

As I left the classroom one day, I found lying on the floor a copy of a text that I had distributed to the students. The text read:

I cannot even understand my own actions. I do not do what I want to do but what I hate. When I act against my own will, by that very fact I agree that the law is good. This indicates that it is not I who do it, but sin which dwells in me. This means that even though I want to do what is right, a law that leads to wrongdoing is always ready at hand. My inner self agrees with the law of God, but I see in my body's members another law at war with the law of my mind; this makes me the prisoner of the law of sin in my members. What a wretched person I am! (Rom 7:15-24)

When I picked up the paper, I noticed in the margin a hastily scrawled note that read, "Mary, this is me!" Two thousand years later, Paul's meditative writing had stirred a young student's soul.

Transcribing a meditative text such as this often allows it to stir us more deeply than just reading the text quietly to ourselves would have. It can also allow us to discover much more in the text than we did by merely reading it. Writing out a text with inner attentiveness often enables it to become more a part of us, and unites us with its meaning and author in a deeply personal way.

In the process, our soul stirrings may lead some of us to copy out the text as beautifully as we can, enlarging and coloring the words and letters that touch us most. This is another classical way of dwelling meditatively on a text and taking it to heart. In doing so, we become part of a long meditative tradition of illuminating soul-stirring texts. We may then begin to understand why the ancient monasteries placed such importance on this kind of meditative writing and why a special room, called the *scriptorium,* or "writing place," was set aside especially for this purpose. This is the kind of meditative writing Master Kosen was practicing when he wrote just three little words with "a mind free from distraction."

I do not know whether she realizes that she is a part of this ancient tradition, but I know a woman who writes her whole personal journal as a beautifully illuminated manuscript. It is her way of honoring the soul stirrings of her life. She does not feel obliged to write everything. A few treasured, soul-stirring words seem to be quite enough.*

As we continue doing this kind of text-based meditative writing, we often find that our writing does not want to stop with literally transcribing or illuminating the original text. The text begins to come alive again. It jumps off the page. It stirs up thoughts, feelings, insights, memories, emotions, and possibilities in us that are not contained in the text itself. At first, we try to catch these in marginal and interlinear notations. Later on, we find that they need much more space. Part of our practice of meditative writing then becomes enlarging on treasured texts and exploring the latent meanings and hidden implications they have for our own lives.

For several years, I studied medieval manuscripts in which I was delighted to see the Judeo-Christian Scriptures begin to come alive in this way. In some manuscripts, the monks, or clerics had added marginal glosses on the text. In other manuscripts, they had added interlinear comments. In still others, they had woven the text and their commentary together in what was sometimes called a *catena aurea,* or "golden chain." Our own attempt to take a treasured text to heart through meditative writing often unfolds in the very same way.

Since we are speaking of meditative writing, it is only natural that we think first of the celebrated sacred texts that, for centuries, have stirred persons' souls. It is important that we not overlook other perhaps less celebrated texts that touch, move, puzzle, and inspire us personally. In this way, they invite us to take them to heart by transcribing them and to discover what they have to say to us.

Along these lines, I think of a woman who came across a story called "The Rainmaker." It is a powerful story about a woman who is able to create harmony and blessing around her, and to

---

*Hannah Hinchman provides a practical and personal introduction to this meditative work of illuminating a text in *A Life in Hand.*

deliver her people from a death-dealing drought, simply by mindfully going about the tasks of her everyday life.

When the woman first came upon this story, she was going through a painful transition in her life. The story came to her as a gift. It moved her deeply, and she felt compelled to copy it in her journal as a way of accepting the gift and taking it to heart. In the middle of her pain, she had finally found a story that spoke of the kind of person she had always wanted to become.

That was years ago. A short time ago, I received a letter from her in which she had copied two commentaries on the story that she had recently come across. The story of "The Rainmaker" clearly continues to stir her soul, and she continues to honor those stirrings by writing her way through them.

As we continue to discover stories, poems, and other texts that have a similar soul-stirring power in our own lives, and as we allow that power to reveal itself in our own handwriting, we begin to realize, without a doubt, that there are many more sacred texts than the religions of this world have been able to codify. As one form of meditative writing, we can then begin to collect our personal treasury of soul-stirring texts, and meditatively to write our way through them. In a very personal sense, they are our scriptures.

Over time, these exercises in meditative writing can make us appreciate, through personal experience, how writing and reading actually are twins. Reading leads to writing and writing leads to reading and both of them are capable of stirring our soul.

A simple exercise that can help us experience how meditative writing and reading go hand in hand is to become quiet and attentively read back to ourselves something that we have written. Such reading can be an extremely important meditative exercise. It can sometimes allow us to discover a truth that we did not even realize or remember that we had written and to experience our souls being stirred by our own writing. As we read what we have written with a meditative attentiveness, it often stirs us to write more. Then we understand what happened to the elderly woman who thought her life had taught her all it had to teach her, until she began reading what she had previously written. Reading and writing are twins.

In addition to reading quietly to ourselves what we have written, a distinct exercise is to read it aloud and, as we do so, to write down whatever our reading aloud stirs up in us. Reading aloud can sometimes stir up feelings and other experiences that can be significantly different from those that we had when we were copying the text or reading it back quietly to ourselves. Then we have something more to note, for we have experienced something more.

For instance, I remember a woman at a workshop who evidently thought that our meditative writing was getting too serious, so she read aloud an entry that she thought would provide us with some comic relief. Half way through her reading, she began to cry. To her amazement, what she thought was funny, as she read it to herself, suddenly felt sad as she read it aloud. She now had something more to write. Writing and reading are twins.

Another classical meditative way of taking a text to heart is one that we currently call "active imagining." It consists in imaginatively placing ourselves in the situation that the text is describing and mentally noting how that feels and what it reveals to us. A variation on this traditional practice involves meditatively speaking with one of the persons in the scene or with the author who stands behind the text.

Both of these ways of imaginatively entering and internalizing a text can be considerably enhanced by doing them as an exercise in meditative writing. Since what happens in such imagining and inner conversations can sometimes be very subtle, writing them down can make them more tangible. It can also reveal the continuity that underlies this kind of meditative work and allow its inner meaning to reveal itself to us over time.

These are but a few of the many ways in which the practice of meditative writing can help us take soul-stirring texts to heart.

Attending to the Present

hether they focus on texts or not, most meditative practices focus on helping us develop a wholehearted attentiveness to the present. In some practices, the focus of our attention may be outward, as when we meditate on a stone, an icon, the movement of our body, or a scene from nature. In other practices, the focus of our attention may be inward, as when we meditate on our thoughts, feelings, dreams, beliefs, and values. In still other practices, the focus of our attention may be both outward *and* inward. An example of this is the meditative practice of examining our conscience, or consciousness. This practice is an exercise in two-dimensional awareness. It involves meditatively attending to the intention with which we began the day while reviewing the way in which our day actually unfolded.

If we already meditate in any of the above ways, we can get started in meditative writing simply by writing as we do so. If we do not meditate in these ways, a helpful way of becoming attentive to the present might be to date a new page in our notebook, become quiet, and write a brief description of how our life has unfolded both outwardly and inwardly in the past twenty-four hours and how we feel about it.

This exercise is a way of becoming attentive not only to the facts but also to the movement of our present experience, and of becoming more sensitive not only to *what* moves us but also to *how* it moves. We can then apply this same attentiveness to describing in writing some of the other outer realities and inner concerns that we experience at present.*

---

*For examples and detailed descriptions of such exercises, see Ira Progoff, *At a Journal Workshop,* pp. 46–56, 65–72, 232–40, and 359–63.

With a little practice, we may discover that, regardless of what our focus may be, describing in writing whatever we notice, just as it comes to us, can help deepen our meditative attentiveness and root our awareness resolutely in the present. It can help us live more attentively than we may have been accustomed to living before.

These exercises in attending to the present can have the added advantage of rooting us firmly in our own experience. So much of our initial education and meditative training is based on the experience and thought of others that we sometimes mistake their experience for our own. Doing so alienates us from our own experience and makes us distrustful of it. Against that background, these exercises in meditative writing have a special importance. They keep us in touch with the reality of our own experience.

Re-membering Our Past

e do not have to be following a particular meditative practice to discover how being attentive to our present experience often reminds us of our past. Some of the memories that come back to us we welcome wholeheartedly; others, we wish we had never remembered. Welcome or not, all of these experiences are part of our lives. When we remember them, it is often a sign that they now have something more to say to us.

Some of these memories come back to us so powerfully that we think we will never forget them. If we do not take the time to write them down, however, they often pass into oblivion again.

Simply writing down memories as they come to us, without analyzing or judging them, can be an important life-based meditative practice. It can make us attentive not only to working with our own lives but also to the many ways in which our life tries to re-member itself.

Hyphenating the word "re-member" graphically reflects what meditatively working with our memories can often involve. It can involve literally "re-membering" parts of our lives which have become *dis-membered,* or disconnected through our inattention or forgetfulness. It can involve honoring the vital connections between our memories, the reality of our present experience, and our future possibilities.

"Re-membering" in this way moves us forward as well as backward. It moves us from our past through our present into the future. It is creative. As memories come back to us, they come back to become part of our life, not just as it was, but also as it now is, and as it may become. In addition, they often reveal a meaning and a purpose that we failed to perceive originally. Perhaps this is why so many spiritual traditions place such strong emphasis on the importance of meditatively "re-membering" the past. It can stir our souls.

Some of the memories that come back to us seem quite content to be briefly noted. They carry little energy. Others, however, are full of energy. They stir us to reenter them meditatively, to describe them in greater detail, and to explore how they may be connected with what we are presently experiencing and with what our lives are yet to become.

As our meditative writing begins to expand in this way, it often takes on a creative vitality of its own. We then personally discover how actively re-membering our past through meditative writing can gradually lead to re-membering the many dimensions of our lives as a whole: past, present, future, inside, outside, personal, and more-than-personal. As we honor our past experiences in this way, memories can sometimes stir us so deeply that they can become some of our most effective teachers.

A good way to get started in re-membering our lives through meditative writing is by opening a new page in our notebook, dating it, becoming quiet, allowing a free-flowing flood of memories to come back to us from different times in our lives, and briefly noting the memories as they come back. We will then have the beginnings of a kind of scrapbook of random memories to which we can add from time to time. As some of these memories continue to call for our attention by continually coming back to us or by becoming increasingly charged emotionally, we can work more intensely with them in our meditative writing.

Another way of re-membering our past is to date a new page in our notebook, become quiet, and allow the chapter headings of our personal or spiritual autobiography to come back to us in whatever way they will. Since we are doing this meditative writing for our own eyes only, we do not edit these chapter headings for public consumption. We simply let them come to us as spontaneously as possible. It is then helpful to read these chapter headings back to ourselves, either quietly or aloud, and to note whatever else they stir up in us.*

---

*Ira Progoff calls this important exercise "Steppingstones." He gives a detailed description of it in several different contexts in *At a Journal Workshop,* pp. 76–101, 134–36, 267, and 279.

As simple as it may seem to be, this little exercise can be foundational for our practice of meditative writing. It can give us a sense of the uniqueness of our own life story, help us honor the inner boundaries between our own life and the lives of others, open our meditative work to our life as a whole, provide us with a fresh, open-ended perspective on the movement and timing of our life, and set a broad, personal context for doing further work in creatively re-membering through meditative writing.

Re-membering Our Dreams

any spiritual traditions place a very special importance on dreaming. It is considered to be a privileged way in which our soul stirs and in which the divine intentions at work in our lives are manifested. The Bible itself is full of accounts of soul-stirring dreams. Psychologists reinforce this tradition by speaking of dreaming as the "royal road" to our inner world and to the deeper-than-conscious reality of our lives.

It is unfortunate, therefore, but not surprising that many of us cannot remember our dreams. Our dreams take place on the inside. They unfold at a deeper-than-conscious level of our lives. They also unfold in a symbolic way that, while it is the primary language of our soul, strikes our daytime "bold pupil" as stupid. Becoming attentive to our dreaming is like going to a strange country where a very strange language is being spoken. It takes courage to go there and stay there. If we listen to many spiritual traditions and modern psychologists, however, the trip is well worth the time and effort. It can put us in touch with our soul.

I remember taking an American tourist around Paris for an afternoon on her brief trip to France. As we finished the tour, I asked her what she thought of Paris.

"These French are so independent," she said, with a certain disdain.

"What do you mean, 'independent'?" I asked.

"All of these signs are in French!" she replied.

Many of us have a similar reaction to our first brief visits to dreamland. Our meditative writing helps change this judgmental reaction by encouraging us to approach our dreaming with a beginner's mind. It can let us meet our dreams on their own ground, taking them for what they are, without trying to analyze, judge, or force them to "make sense" in the language of our conscious minds. It can allow us to experience our dreams as they are, so that they may begin communicating with us on their own terms, giving us a feel for their rich symbolic language.

Although we are often not aware of it, the meditative writing that we do in other areas of our lives has a way of gradually preparing us for re-membering our dreams. For one thing, it gives us a habit of honoring our experience for what it is. For another, our meditative writing often takes us to the deeper-than-conscious place from which dreaming comes, and introduces us to the symbolic language that is common to the daydreaming, imagining, fantasizing, and meditating that go in that place. This is the same language in which our dreaming expresses itself. In these ways, our meditative writing gradually prepares us for remembering our dreaming.

Two or three days into some of the retreats and workshops that I give in meditative writing, I often invite the participants to be attentive to whether or not they have any dreams that night. Even people who "have never had a dream in their lives" often come back the next day with a few dreams which they have recorded. Their meditative writing had prepared them for remembering their dreams.

Meditative writing, then, can be a way of creatively remembering our dreaming. First of all, the process of writing itself can sometimes let us remember a whole dream, when all that we had remembered before beginning to write was a fragment of it. In addition, our writing does not merely reconstruct dreams we *have had*. It recalls them in present time and therefore allows them to connect to our present experience. This, in itself, is a creative move. Finally, our meditative writing can also help us creatively "re-member" our dreaming by revealing how our dreams connect with one another and with the movement of our lives as a whole. As we allow our dreaming to come alive for us and to move through our whole lives in this soul-stirring way, we get a felt sense of what our dreaming is really all about. Then we are no longer foreigners in dreamland. We recognize that what goes on there is part of our life and that the language of our dreaming is the primary language of our soul.

A simple first step in this work of creatively remembering our dreams is the exercise of recording the dreams that we are currently having. If we have never done this before, some of the basic hints that can help get us started are:

- keeping our notebook open by the bed, with a pen and a lamp conveniently nearby;
- making a resolution before retiring to welcome dreams and record them;
- recording dreams as soon as we wake up;
- recording fragments of dreams, since the meditative writing itself frequently recalls other parts of them;
- not getting up right away, but spending some time in a half-awake state recalling any dreaming that may have gone on;
- being open to making at least brief dream entries if we are awakened during the night;
- experimenting with keeping a voice-activated tape recorder by the bed to record dreams verbally for later meditative writing.

Taking time to record our dreams is an important first step toward learning how to work actively with them and allowing them to reconnect with our life as a whole through our practice of meditative writing. Recording our dreams can open the door for us to a very important area of meditative work.*

---

*Two fine guides in the more subtle and advanced aspects of working with dreams are Robert Johnson in *Inner Work* and Ira Progoff in *At a Journal Workshop,* pp. 196–221. Tristine Rainer provides a brief introduction to dream work in *The New Diary,* chap. 8.

Creatively Forgetting

ake a walk." In several traditions, this advice can be an invitation to yet another meditative practice: walking meditation. It consists essentially in walking with a heightened attentiveness to all that is going on around and within us. It is sometimes called "walking in mindfulness." It often follows a time of prolonged sitting meditation. In this context, it also serves as a meditative "break" and as a way of taking our deepened meditative attentiveness *on the road*.

Walking meditation is another way in which meditative practice imitates life. It is quite natural, from time to time, for us to "take a walk," not only to stretch our legs but also to stretch our minds and to get some salutary distance from what we have been trying too hard to do.

When we get so caught up in meditative writing that we think we cannot afford the time to take a walk, then from the point of view of cultivating our soul, the advice "take a walk" becomes doubly important for us. Perhaps without realizing it, we are beginning to presume that if we do not do our soul work—and do it *now*—it will not get done. In the long run, that attitude is always destructive of the soul. It presumes that our soul is completely under our control and reduces it to the sum total of our conscious actions.

Our soul is much bigger than that. It works at much deeper than conscious levels and responds most creatively when we willingly entrust it with our conscious concerns, rather than compulsively reduce it to one of them. Walking meditation is one way in which we can entrust our conscious concerns to our soul and forget about them for a while. Our soul is then free to work on them as it sees fit. Its creativity does not depend on our "bold pupil" presence.

In a similar way, we honor how the soul works when, having puzzled over a certain concern for a while, we say, "I'll sleep on it." In "sleeping on it," we are actually making a very natural meditative move. We are entrusting our concerns to our soul and giving it time to ratify, reverse, illuminate, or modify them as it will. We would not be the first one to have a dream creatively illuminate one of our most urgent concerns while we were just "sleeping on it."

Recently, I have been working as a spiritual director in a therapeutic center in which most of the guests work very intensely trying to sort out the personal difficulties that they are experiencing. For many of them, walking becomes one of their primary ways of meditating. While they are walking, they begin to forget about all the analytic work they are doing. Their minds relax and sometimes become free to receive some of their most important soul stirrings. Often without even knowing that they are meditating, they become part of the very long tradition of meditative walking.

When we first start practicing meditative writing, we often do so with the intention of "getting things out on paper" and remembering parts of our lives that we may have forgotten or overlooked. This is good, as far as it goes. When it goes as far as it wants to, however, our writing often begins to introduce us to how it can be a channel for creatively forgetting.

Our first intimation of this often comes when we know with certainty that we have written something yet we are unable to find it. At first, we are often frustrated by this experience. If we can patiently stay with it, however, we begin to recognize the advantage writing allows us of writing things down not only to remember them but also to creatively forget them. Then our minds are free to move on to other experiences. When we allow our minds to be free in this way, we often come across quite gracefully what we had been looking for quite frantically. When we do so, it often presents itself to us in a context that surprises and enlightens us. It is as though it wanted to be creatively forgotten so that it could creatively remember itself when the right time came.

It often takes some practice in meditative writing to get the full gist of how writing's capacity for creative forgetting actually works, and how it mirrors a basic dynamic of the soul. If we want to experiment a bit with this, a good way to begin is to open our notebook, write the current date on a page, take some time to become quiet, and briefly describe something that deeply concerns or puzzles us. Even though we may want to resolve it then and there, once and for all, we "forget about it" and take a walk.

As we walk, we remain attentive to what is going on around us as well as what is going on within us. Along the way, we might even jot down some key-word notes to make us even more attentive. Afterward, we describe what came to us while we walked, being attentive to how it may or may not relate to the concern on which we had previously focused.*

In addition to being a channel for creatively remembering, meditative writing can also be a channel for creatively forgetting and allowing our soul to continue to do its work in silence.

---

*For a personal and most engaging commentary on the connection between walking meditation and creative writing, see Burghild Nina Holzer's *A Walk Between Heaven and Earth*.

Relating Soulfully

n many meditative traditions, meeting with a guide or companion who can help us discern and cultivate the stirrings of our own soul is an important part of living meditatively. Within the various traditions, the names of such guides vary. They are called guru, rabbi, shaman, starets, abba, amma, spiritual mother, spiritual father, philosopher, teacher, master, abbot, doctor, healer, medicine man, priest, medicine woman, bodhisattva, or spiritual director, to mention just a few of the names. Their basic work, however, is very much the same. It is to relate to others soulfully as they accompany them on their inner journeys.

In modern times, many of us add "psychologist" to this list, when we discover a compassionate psychotherapist (which literally means "soul healer") who can help us honestly get in touch with the inner and outer realities of our lives.

If we are already meeting with a spiritual director, counselor, or psychotherapist, that work can be yet another channel for helpful exercises in meditative writing. We can devote part of our meditative writing to keeping a written account of our meetings, what is said, and what that stirs up in us. We can also begin to explore the implications of some of the things we are discovering about ourselves through these meetings. It is common for such guides to suggest things for us to consider, read, or do. We can also incorporate such suggestions, together with their effects and outcomes, into our practice of meditative writing.

Another way to deepen our work with our therapist or spiritual director is to meet with them not only face to face but also heart to heart, through our meditative writing. To do this, we put the date on a new page of our notebook, become quiet, meet inwardly with the other person and let a free-floating conversation unfold between us, writing down what each of us is led to say and whatever else we may notice, just as it comes to us. We then gradually come away from this inner meeting, and if we have time, read what we have written and note any additional observations that may come to mind.

At first, such inner meetings may seem unreal and somewhat contrived to us. We often spend much of the time trying to figure out what our therapist or spiritual director would "really" say, were we to say this or that to them. At this stage, we are not yet trusting the reality of our inner experience. As our inner meetings become more deeply relaxed and meditative, we begin to feel much more at home in this inner work and to experience its inherent reality and value. These meetings then become a concrete way in which we can experience the guidance that is always available within us. We may then begin to realize that this is the same inner guidance to which our teachers, therapists, and spiritual directors have been trying to introduce us.

When we describe meeting inwardly with another person as a meditative exercise, it may seem far removed from our ordinary experience. Actually, this formal exercise builds on a very common experience that often goes on quite spontaneously within us. How often do we find ourselves caught up in a kind of "inner chatter" with persons of importance in our lives? How often do we find ourselves thinking, wondering, fantasizing, and dreaming about them? How often does our mental prayer spontaneously take the form of a personal conversation with the person to whom we are praying? Meeting inwardly with another person may not be as far removed from our personal experience as we may think.

Incorporating into our practice of meditative writing the experiences of "inner chatter" that go on spontaneously within us is a way of honoring them. It is also a way of allowing them to move beyond the vicious circles in which they customarily move and become mutual, person-to-person, rather than person-to-object, relationships. It can also help us discover that, in the work of soul stirring, some of our most important guides are not outside of us but within us.

In his fourth-century soliloquies, Augustine of Hippo lets us see this discovery actually happening, in what may be seen as a keynote for meditative writing:

> When I had been pondering many different things to myself for a long time, and had for many days been seeking my own self and what my own good was, and what evil was to be avoided, there suddenly spoke to me—what was it? I myself or someone else, inside me or outside me? (this is the very thing I would love to know but don't)—at any rate, Reason said to me:
>
> *Reason:* Look, suppose you had discovered something: to whom would you entrust your discovery, so that you might move on to other matters?
>
> *Augustine:* To memory, of course.
>
> *Reason:* And is memory so powerful that it can preserve properly everything that has been thought out?
>
> *Augustine:* That is a difficult thing to do, indeed: impossible, in fact.
>
> *Reason:* One must, therefore, write it down. But what are you going to do, seeing that your health will not allow the hard work involved in writing? For these things should not be dictated: they demand absolute privacy.
>
> *Augustine:* You're quite right. I really don't know what I am to do.
>
> *Reason:* Pray for health, and help, so that you might achieve your aims, and see to it that the prayer is written down, so that you might derive more courage from what you have yourself produced. Then summarize what you have discovered in a few brief concluding remarks. And don't bother to look for the encouragement of a large number of readers: if there is something for a few of your fellow citizens, that will be enough.
>
> *Augustine:* I'll do that....*

---

*Saint Augustine, *Soliloquies and Immortality of the Soul*, trans. Gerard Watson (Warminster, England: Aris and Phillips, 1990), p. 23.

That is exactly what Augustine continued to do, not only in the extended dialogue with God that ensued, but in the over forty years of meditative writing through which he followed up on this experience.

A simple way to follow Augustine's lead in meditative writing and to take an important step toward meeting with an inner guide is to make a list of the guides we have known. To do this, we date a new page in our notebook, become quiet, and allow ourselves to remember and list the names of persons who have been or can be inner guides for us. When we finish writing, we quietly read what we have written, adding whatever else comes to mind as we do so.

As we read it back to ourselves, this list can often surprise us. It can include persons from any time and culture, living or dead, celebrated or unknown, as well as mythic and divine figures. It can reflect the scope and character of our deepest searching. It can also reflect the sometimes overlooked support we have had on that journey, and serve as a gathering place for the many inner guides we have known along the way. As additional names come to mind later on, we can add them to our list. Just doing that can be a way of communing with them and honoring their presence in our lives.

Another exercise in meditative writing is to meet inwardly with one of the guides whom we have listed. To do so, we place the date on a new page in our notebook, keep in mind the name of the person with whom we feel called to meet, and allow ourselves to become quiet so that we may meet in a place that is deeper than our customary thinking. If feelings and images emerge as we go to the place of inner meeting, we record them as an integral part of the meditative experience. We then allow ourselves to become inwardly present to the other person. We write down whatever we feel moved to say to them as well as whatever they may have to say to us. We do this for as long as we have time, or for as long as it feels comfortable. Afterward, we read to ourselves what we have written and note whatever else it stirs up in us.

It is important that we come away from this exercise gradually and attentively, just as we would from any meeting with a person and from any meditative exercise. This gives us time to adjust to what might be a different atmosphere between our inner and outer experience, and it allows us to be more sensitive to the more subtle stirrings that often come to us as we emerge from meditative experiences of this kind.

It sometimes takes several attempts before we become comfortable with meeting with another person in this way. As we become more comfortable with them, these inner meetings often take on a life of their own. They then develop a meditative atmosphere and depth that are often lacking in our spontaneous "inner chatter," and a mutuality that is frequently missing in our one-sided ways of praying.

I remember a very empirically minded engineer for whom the whole notion of meeting with an inner guide seemed utterly ridiculous. He was an adamant extrovert, but he was empirically minded enough to try his hand at the exercise. He wrote a meditative dialogue with Johann Sebastian Bach, whose music had been a source of great strength and inspiration to him at difficult times in his life. He was surprised by how naturally his writing flowed, and by the depth of what it revealed to him. He read it back to me privately, with tears in his eyes.

As he finished reading, he slammed his journal shut and said, "And that's real, damn it!"

I smiled. "Welcome to the empiricism of the soul," I thought to myself.

Meeting with an inner guide had stirred his soul, and he was not about to deny it.

In a similar way, meditative writing can become a pathway for each of us to an "empiricism of our soul" that eventually makes the reality of our inner life undeniable. I know some persons for whom meeting with an inner guide in the way we have just described has become one of their primary meditative practices. It has become a wellspring of wisdom for them, as they seek to live with soulful integrity.

As our practice of meditative writing leads us to become "empiricists of the soul" through this kind of meditative meeting, a very important change often begins to take place in our face-to-face meetings with our counselors, therapists, or spiritual directors. We become more personally caught up in the experiment of our lives, and much more personally involved in it than our guides may be. Formerly, we may have waited passively for directions or answers from them, or put a lot of energy into defending ourselves from being perceived as we really are. Now, we take the initiative, "telling it like it is" and weighing our guide's comments against the reality of our own inner experience. This change marks a critically important turning point in our inner work.

As a spiritual director, I have seen this change take place in many persons' lives. It is very beautiful to see. It marks a turning point in their spiritual journeys, in which the energy, involvement, vitality, direction, and wisdom begin coming to them from the inside out.

Of course, there is much more involved in the practice of inner meeting than we have been able to describe here. These few suggestions can help us get started, however, in this important kind of meditative work.†

---

†Ira Progoff provides careful guidance in this kind of work in *At a Journal Workshop,* pp. 127–40 and 267–85, and extends it to other key areas of life in describing dialogues with works, body, events, and society, pp. 123–94.

Working with SoulStirring Phrases

any spiritual traditions place a special emphasis on meditating with small prayer phrases that can stir our souls and keep us in touch throughout the day with the reality of our soul, which we have experienced while meditating. "Mantras," "prayer phrases," "ejaculations," "aspirations," "affirmations," and "spiritual bouquets," are a few of the many names used for such phrases. They are often emotionally charged summaries of a guide's wisdom, a treasured text, a deeply felt truth, or a personal experience.

"Pray for health, and help, so that you might achieve your aims, and see to it that the prayer is written down, so that you might derive more courage from what you have yourself produced," Augustine's inner voice suggests to him, in the text we have already cited.

After taking the advice and writing for about eight pages, Augustine returns to the inner dialogue:

Augustine: So, I have prayed to God.
Reason: What then do you want to know?
Augustine: All these things that I have prayed for.
Reason: Sum them up briefly.
Augustine: I want to know God and the soul.

Augustine would spend the rest of his life exploring this desire. Were he to have put it in the classic form of a soul-stirring prayer phrase, it might have been something like "Knowing my God and my soul." Much of Augustine's subsequent meditative writing would flow from the desire carried in this little phrase. In the same way, all of his theological writing flows from another of his soul-stirring phrases: "faith seeking understanding."

Some of these soul-stirring phrases, may come to us from hymns, poems, prayers, and classical religious traditions, such as:

Baruch Atah Adonai....Blessed be the Lord our God....
  (The beginning of many Hebrew prayers.)

In the secret of my heart....
  (A phrase from Psalm 50:8.)

Whose love endures forever....
  (A phrase from Psalm 118:1.)

Loving God with all my heart....
  (A paraphrase of the great commandment, Deuteronomy 6:5.)

The light shines on in darkness....
  (A phrase from the Gospel of John 1:5.)

Kyrie Eleison....Lord Jesus Christ have mercy....;
  (The "Jesus Prayer" from the Roman Catholic mass.)

One in mind and one in heart....
  (A paraphrase from Saint Augustine's monastic rule.)

Walking in a sacred way....
  (A Native-American expression.)

Ego vobis; vos mihi....I am yours and you are mine....
  (The motto of an ancient monastic community.)

Brother sun and sister moon....
  (A paraphrase from Saint Francis's Canticle to the Sun.)

Like a motherless child....
  (A phrase from a Negro spiritual.)

Like shining from shook foil....
  (A phrase from Gerard Manley Hopkins's poem, "God's Grandeur.")

Other soul-stirring phrases come to us from our personal experience or our own meditative practice:

Something good will come of this....

In the center of the storm....

Letting go and letting God....

In the shadow of the cross....

The ending of a season....

Following the narrow path....

In the chapel of my heart....

The Mystery unfolding....

The ebb and flow of living....

Since many of us may *think* that we are living prosaic lives, we often consider soul-stirring phrases such as these to be beyond us. As we continue to practice meditative writing, however, we often find little poetic phrases such as these coming to us quite spontaneously. When soul-stirring phrases first come to some of the people with whom I work in spiritual direction, they often excuse themselves before reading them to me by saying, "I'm not a poet, but this came to me...."

I have to smile when they say this. It means that their thinking has not yet caught up with their meditative experience. Like a lover running before the clock, their meditating is out ahead of their thinking. It is introducing them to the deeply moving, poetic language of their soul.

If we are presently accustomed to meditating with soul-stirring phrases in some form of mantra meditation or centering prayer, we can complement and enhance that work by describing it in writing, either while we are meditating or shortly after we finish.

In time, we will have a written record of where such phrases take us, what they reveal to us along the way, and how they relate to our life as a whole. We will also have a personal source from which additional prayer phrases and meditative experiences often come.

If we are unfamiliar with such meditative work, but would like to make it part of our experiment in meditative writing, the following exercise might be helpful as a start. We write the date on a new page in our notebooks, become quiet, let a list of experiences that have stirred our soul and the phrases that reflect them come to mind, and record them as they come. Some of these phrases may come from treasured texts and hymns, for this is another way of taking texts to heart. Others will come from our personal experiences. If we have already done some meditative writing, we might review that to see if it contains any soul-stirring phrases that we may have overlooked when we wrote them.

If, whenever we are touched by a soul-stirring phrase or experience, we add it to our list, in time our list itself can become a soul-stirring reflection of our search for what we most deeply desire. As we read it back to ourselves, we often experience it as a pathway of soul-stirring moments that have marked our spiritual journey. In addition, the individual entries can become springboards for additional meditative experiences in our ongoing practice of meditative writing.

If we want to experiment with the above exercise, even before we have our own list of soul-stirring phrases we can write the date on a new page of our notebook, become quiet, slowly reread the soul-stirring phrases that are listed above, and note whatever they stir up in us and how they relate to one another. As we do so, additional soul-stirring experiences or phrases often come to mind. We can then record them as a way of beginning our own list.

I am currently working in spiritual direction with a man who has been guided by one soul-stirring phrase for several years. It has become a dear friend and teacher for him. It continually stirs his soul, and speaks to his life in ways that often surprise him. As his relationship with it continues to unfold, this phase has become the pedal point of his spiritual journey. It has begun to knit together the depths and the surface, the inner and outer, and the quiet and active dimensions of his life.

There is much more involved in the practice of meditatively working with soul-stirring phrases than we have been able to suggest here. What we have described is enough to get us started. If we feel drawn by that experience to pursue this important channel of meditative work further, Ira Progoff provides us with masterful guidance as he ingeniously interweaves the wisdom of this ancient tradition of meditation, the discoveries of modern psychology, and the practice of meditative writing.*

Another rich resource for our meditative work with soul-stirring phrases is Robert Morneau's series of books on mantric prayer.† These small books contain a wealth of material for mantra meditation presented in a way that allows us to experience the holistic nature of such prayer and how it can move, quite spontaneously, from repeating a soul-stirring phrase, to savoring the text from which it comes, to meditatively reflecting and enlarging on the text and our own experience, to creating or dwelling on a picture or icon, to singing refrains, to summarizing our experience in a personal prayer. This description itself should be enough to give us a sense of the rich potential of meditative writing as a way of working with soul-stirring phrases.

---

*See *The Well and the Cathedral* and *At a Journal Workshop*, pp. 312-49 and 392-96.

†See *Mantras for the Morning*, *Mantras for the Evening*, and *Mantras for the Midnight*.

Moving Beyond Words

"he one who speaks, does not know. The one who knows, does not speak."

This chastening saying of the Chinese sage Lao Tzu reminds us of the importance that most spiritual traditions place on silence. "Letting silence speak the word" is a prayer phrase of one of my retreatants that reflects one side of that tradition. "Letting words flow to silence" is a prayer phrase that can reflect the other side. Within these traditions, it is as though words are most faithful when they honestly reflect the silence from which they come and courageously reach for the silence into which they go.

The same seems to be true of meditative writing. It comes from the silence that gives birth to soul-stirring words. That is one reason why we always begin our exercises in meditative writing by becoming quiet.

Meditative writing also flows toward a silence that is much bigger than words. As our meditative writing approaches the silence that is bigger than words, our writing begins to run out and the quiet eloquence of living meditatively begins to take over.

One way in which meditative writing spontaneously moves us beyond words is that it gives us inner images that, as the saying goes, are worth a thousand words. When we are in a writing frame of mind, we often begin by trying to describe these images in words. Another way to go, however, is to allow our writing to move beyond words by drawing the images as they come to us. In doing so, we personally become part of yet another ancient meditative tradition: meditating with icons or drawn images.

I know a woman whose meditative writing increasingly began to take the form of simple, poetic prayer phrases. After a while, these phrases were accompanied by inner images that she drew as part of her meditative writing practice. The images meant more to her than she could say. They were soul-stirring images that moved her very deeply.

Since she thought that she was not an artist, she enrolled in a course at a local college in order to learn to draw. Before long, she dropped the course, realizing that she was being called to allow her meditative writing to teach her to draw, not to try to become a professional artist.

Once again, I had to smile. Here was another person whose meditative work was out ahead of her thinking. She *thought* she was not an artist, but here she was, doing Blake-like drawings of her soul-stirring experiences.

When things are getting so verbose as to become uncommunicative, we sometimes say, "Draw me a picture." The same can be true in our practice of meditative writing. At times, we can let it take the form of doodling, drawing, or painting.

"Draw me a picture," can also lead us to two other exercises in meditative writing.

The first exercise is called "clustering." It is quite common among speed readers and diarists. It involves drawing a key-word-picture that reflects the way in which we see things to be interconnected. This exercise can allow us to visualize and remember complex networks of thought and experience, somewhat as a chemist would visualize the structure of a molecule. Our drawings often wind up looking like a word tree with key-words branching out from one another in several directions.*

Were we to do a "clustering" exercise on the key topics in this whole section on practicing meditative writing, it would look something like this:

The second exercise in meditative drawing that we may want to try is called "mandala meditation." It involves drawing or painting a circular or square picture of what our life feels like at the present time. As we continue to do drawings of this kind, they can provide us with a series of overlays that symbolically reflect not only isolated times in the movement of our lives but also the inner continuity of our lives unfolding. The snapshots of our individual mandala drawings then become a moving picture of our life. By working with mandalas, we become part of a very ancient meditative tradition of symbolically expressing the reality of our life by drawing images.†

Another way of moving beyond words in our meditative writing is by becoming attentive to the silence that is before, beneath, and between our words both as we write and as we read back to ourselves what we have written. This exercise allows us to become more attentive to the silence into which our writing sometimes leads us. When we feel our writing taking us into the silence, we

---

*On the technique of clustering, see Tristine Rainer, *The New Diary,* chap. 9, and pp. 83–87 for the related technique of drawing maps of consciousness.

†Susanne Fincher provides a comprehensive guide to this kind of work in *Creating Mandalas for Insight, Healing, and Self-Expression.* See also Lucia Carpacione, *The Creative Journal.* On experiencing painting as a reflection of the soul, see Peter Rogers's *A Painter's Quest* and Sister Wendy Beckett's *The Gaze of Love.*

simply go there and allow ourselves to be in the silence, "letting words flow to silence...." When we become aware of something stirring in the silence, we then record it, "letting silence speak the word...."

I once worked with a Hasidic storyteller who sometimes began his storytelling sessions by singing, "You can learn a lot from my words. You can learn a lot from the tone of my voice. But you can learn much more —you can learn *much* more —from the silence between my words."

The same is true of our meditative writing. Sometimes it is only in reading our written meditations back to ourselves that we are able to experience the silence between our words and how much it has to reveal.

For some of us, this exercise in attending to the silence is not as easy as it sounds. We are frightened by sitting in silence. It makes us feel uneasy. It often makes us feel anxious and guilty as well. We feel as though we should be doing something, namely writing. Nevertheless, when our writing takes us to this place beyond words, that is where we are meant to be.

I sometimes try to console people who complain about being frightened and disappointed when their writing spontaneously leads them into a deep inner silence. "Nothing is coming," they complain.

"Don't feel bad," I reply. "It sometimes takes people years of meditative practice to get to that silence."

As true as it is, my jest does little to console them. That is understandable. Nothing someone *says* will let us discover the richness of this kind of silence. Only the silence itself can do that. If we want to discover that richness, we will simply have to allow ourselves to experience the silence into which meditative writing sometimes leads us.

"Letting words flow to silence..."

Clarifying Our Values and Beliefs

fter years of dedicated inner work, and often on the other side of the kind of silence that we have been describing, the leaders and participants in many meditative, spiritual, philosophical, and political traditions are led to sum up what they have discovered along the way for their own and others' benefit.

Augustine's inner voice advises him: "....Then summarize what you have discovered in a few brief concluding remarks. And don't bother to look for the encouragement of a large number of readers: if there is something for a few of your fellow citizens, that will be enough."

"I'll do that," he responds. And he does it.

When we spoke of taking texts to heart, we described several ways in which we can make such teachings the subject for some of our meditative writing. Even more importantly, such teachings can invite us to join in a similar soul-stirring work ourselves. They can invite us to sum up, from time to time, what we have discovered through our practice of meditative writing in order to clarify what we most deeply believe and value. They can invite us to articulate our personal code, cult, and creed—our own "rule of life." They can invite us to change "We hold these truths to be self-evident..." to "I hold these truths to be self-evident..." and to fill in the blanks.

When the time comes in our own inner work, meditative writing can be a helpful tool for clarifying and exploring our beliefs and values, in whatever form our life suggests that we do so. Since these entries are not written in stone, they can continue to change and grow as our life and meditative work go on. As we continue to add to these entries, they in turn often begin to lend a deeper meditative quality and clarity to *how* our life and work goes on.

In order to get started in this aspect of our meditative work, we can write the date on a new page in our notebook, become quiet, and briefly describe in a paragraph or two what we truly believe and value at this time in our lives and what has led us to do so.

This initial entry can serve to open the door to this area of our meditative writing. As we feel led to do so, we can follow it with additional entries drawn from our own experience and meditative practice or from other sources that reflect our deepest values and beliefs.*

It is often from this place in our meditative writing that we may be led to write a spiritual autobiography or a personal journal in order to share our deepest values with our family and friends, just as Augustine did in writing his *Confessions*. In the process, we would be further clarifying our own values and beliefs and joining a very long and rich tradition of meditative writing.†

---

*For a more detailed description of how to do this work, see Progoff's *At a Journal Workshop,* pp. 310-11 and 350-58, and both volumes of George Simons's *Journal for Life.* See also Tristine Rainer's description of the technique of list-making in *The New Diary,* pp. 72-79.

†Examples of this kind of work abound. For some guidance in doing it, see Lois Daniel, *How to Write Your Own Life Story,* Sam Keen and Anne Valley-Fox's *Your Mythic Journey,* and Christian Hageseth III's *A Thirteen Moon Journal.*

Living Soulfully

f we get too serious about meditative writing, we can begin to confuse it with living. Then we can begin to think that meditative writing is about *keeping* a journal. That is when our meditative writing often begins to tell us in many different ways, "Take a break," or "Take a walk," or "Get a life!"

This is very good advice. It echoes an old Latin adage, "Live first and then philosophize." This proverb applies well to any life-based way of meditating: "Live first and then meditate." As a life-based way of meditating, our soul-stirring writing is not merely about writing. It is about living soulfully. It helps us develop the attentiveness, skills, and discipline to note and follow the stirrings of our soul in writing so that we may be able more gracefully to note and follow the stirrings of our soul in our everyday lives.

All of the ways of practicing meditative writing that we have described in this section are ways of moving us toward living soulfully. We can make that fact the subject of a distinct exercise in meditative writing by devoting one of our meditative sessions to noting whether or not our practice of meditative writing is enabling us to live more sensitive, creative, wise, and soulful lives. In the end, that is what this book and all the ways of practicing meditative writing that we have described are really all about: living soulfully.

EPILOGUE

n the wake of the story about how the words "The First Principle" were originally written, we have described the process, the character, and some ways of practicing meditative writing. We may now have a much better sense of how meditative writing can become a soul-stirring gateway through which we can pass from the marketplace to the inner temple of our lives, and from the inner temple to the marketplace, again and again.

As we practice meditative writing in this spirit, from time to time we too may experience ourselves, our writing, and our meditating becoming one. Then, as docile pupils of Master Kosen, we may find the soul-stirring quality of our writing beginning to overflow into our lives as a whole, just as it did for him.

When this happens, we will know, not from hearsay but from our own experience, what meditative writing is all about. For, when all is said and done, meditative writing is all about living soulfully. Whether our own "bold pupil" agrees or not, when we are engaged in a lifework of this magnitude, we are engaged in a "masterpiece" in process.

Postscripts

Some Background on Meditative Writing

he following is a slightly revised version of an article on spiritual journal writing that I originally had published in the *Westminster Dictionary of Christian Spirituality*. I include it here since it may enrich our personal practice of meditative writing, allowing us to experience it both as an extension of an ancient Judeo-Christian tradition of meditative writing as well as certain modern trends in journaling.

Within the Judeo-Christian tradition, the prototype for meditative writing is the Sacred Scriptures, or "Sacred Writings." These writings reflect the soul-searching of a whole People: its fears, doubts, hopes, struggles, discoveries, and prayers; its most treasured experiences; its time-tested beliefs and traditions; its relationship to God and the world; its innermost sense of life's meaning and purpose. In short, these writings faithfully reflect the story of a believing People's pilgrimage toward God. They are the spiritual journal of a family of faith. Some of these writings take an intimate and highly personal form, such as certain sections from the prophets and psalms and many passages from the letters of Paul. Others take a more objective and even anonymous form, such as some of the historical and legal passages and the synoptic Gospels. However, all of them are recognized by the community of believers as authentic reflections of its spiritual autobiography and as soul-stirring texts.

When the Sacred Scriptures are taken as its prototype, spiritual journal writing takes on a much broader scope than is often attributed to it.

For one thing, regardless of the form it takes, such meditative writing is then seen basically to be an exercise in spiritual autobiography. It is seen to be an honest chronicling of the search for, and discovery of, how God acts in human life.

For another, such meditative writing admits of a multiplicity of purposes, just as the Sacred Scriptures were written sometimes to edify, instruct, correct, or teach others; sometimes to chronicle current events, or to remember or reconstruct past experiences, or to envision an unseen future; and sometimes to plumb the depths of the heart in prayer.

In addition, such meditative writing admits of a multiplicity of literary forms, just as the Sacred Scriptures include stories, prophesies, laws, proverbs, letters, songs, prayers, sermons, dreams, visions, and many other forms.

Finally, such meditative writing is capable of combining, in a symbiotic way, both the secular and the sacred and the personal and the communal, just as the Sacred Scriptures do.

From these characteristics, it can be seen how important it is to keep the prototype of Sacred Scripture in mind if we are to appreciate the full scope of meditative writing as a spiritual discipline.

Among the Fathers of the Church, Saint Augustine best personifies the importance of meditative writing as a discipline for spiritual growth. In his *Soliloquies,* Augustine tells of how an inner voice prompted him to write down his innermost thoughts and discoveries, so that he might become even more animated in his search for truth. When the inner voice finally asks what it is he wishes to know through all of his searching, Augustine replies, "I desire to know God and the soul."

The over eight thousand pages that remain of Augustine's writing over the next four decades of his life attest to how deep this desire to know God and the soul actually went, and to how seriously Augustine took this initial inner prompting to continue his quest and to write down his innermost thoughts and discoveries. The *Confessions* are undoubtedly the most celebrated and influential fruit of Augustine's dedication to the discipline of meditative writing, but they are by no means its only fruit. To the *Confessions* must certainly be added his early apologetic works, his highly personal commentaries on Sacred Scripture, his voluminous correspondence, his homilies, and his *Retractations,* if not his entire *opera omnia.* The life and works of Augustine go hand in hand. For him, meditative writing was not merely one among many literary forms. It was a privileged channel for personal, spiritual, and ministerial growth.

Within the Christian monastic tradition, meditative writing frequently finds its place as a spiritual exercise that expresses the monk's attempts to internalize the Sacred Scriptures. It often takes the form of carefully copied or illuminated texts, prayerful commentaries or sermons on a biblical text, or letters of spiritual direction. Some of the writings of Saint Bernard (1153), William of St. Thierry (1148), and Saint Bonaventure (1274) exemplify this tradition.

Among the mystics, and within the Reformation tradition, the renewed emphasis on personal religious experience gives meditative journal writing a place of special prominence as a spiritual discipline. The journals of the Pilgrims, Puritans, and Quakers (especially George Fox) give eloquent witness to this renewal as well as to the reemergence of the Augustinian model of spiritual autobiography. Other examples include the diaries, autobiographies, or spiritual treatises of Egeria (c. 384), Meister Eckhart (1327-28), Julian of Norwich (1416/23), St. Ignatius of Loyola (1556), St. Teresa of Avila (1582), Blaise Pascal (1662), John Henry Newman (1890), and Thérèse of Lisieux (1897).

The soul searching of the nineteenth and twentieth centuries and the emergence of psychoanalysis have served to highlight the importance of journal writing both as a channel for therapeutic self-understanding and as a distinct literary form. Carl Jung, Marion Milner, and Anaïs Nin were among the leaders in this movement. This development has not taken place, however, without raising some questions among some religious commentators about the spiritual limitations of such writing.

Nevertheless, the second half of the twentieth century has witnessed the beginning of a genuine renaissance in journal writing as a spiritual discipline, in a very broad sense of that word. This renaissance is reflected in journals such as those of Anne Frank, Pope John XXIII, and Dag Hammarskjöld. It is personified in the writings of the late Cistercian monk Thomas Merton. It is mirrored in the publication of an increasing number of diaries and of books and articles on the techniques of journal and diary writing. Even more fundamentally, this renaissance shows promise of being perpetuated by the pioneering work that Ira Progoff has done in developing a comprehensive methodology for journal writing as a discipline for personal, creative, and spiritual growth.

If the long tradition of spiritual journal writing makes one thing eminently clear, it is that writing about what concerns us most can be extremely helpful spiritually. It makes it clear that Franz Kafka was right when he said that writing, itself, is a form of prayer.

Footnote Leads for Further Practice

The footnotes have been clustered here to allow them to reflect the flow of our work and to serve as a convenient springboard for further expanding our practice of meditative writing.

"The First Principle"

*Reps, Paul (ed.), *Zen Flesh, Zen Bones* (New York: Doubleday, n.d.) p. 23.

Expanding Our Practice

*Notable among these are Kathleen Adams's *The Way of the Journal;* Christina Baldwin's *One to One;* Harry J. Cargas's *Keeping a Spiritual Journal;* Sam Keen and Anne Valley-Fox's *Your Mythic Journey;* Morton T. Kelsey's *Adventure Inward;* Ronald Klug's *How to Keep a Spiritual Journal;* Tristine Rainer's *The New Diary,* and Richard Solly and Roseann Lloyd's *Journey Notes.*

Taking Texts to Heart

*Hannah Hinchman provides a practical and personal introduction to this meditative work of illuminating a text in *A Life in Hand.*

Attending to the Present

*For examples and detailed descriptions of such exercises, see Ira Progoff, *At a Journal Workshop,* pp. 46-56, 65-72, 232-40, and 359-63.

Re-membering Our Past

*Ira Progoff calls this important exercise "Steppingstones." He gives a detailed description of it in several different contexts in *At a Journal Workshop*, pp. 76–101, 134–36, 267, and 279.

Re-membering Our Dreams

*Two fine guides in the more subtle and advanced aspects of working with dreams are Robert Johnson in *Inner Work* and Ira Progoff in *At a Journal Workshop*, pp. 196–221. Tristine Rainer provides a brief introduction to dream work in *The New Diary*, chap. 8.

Creatively Forgetting

*For a personal and most engaging commentary on the connection between walking meditation and creative writing, see Burghild Nina Holzer's *A Walk Between Heaven and Earth*.

Relating Soulfully

*Saint Augustine, *Soliloquies and Immortality of the Soul*, trans. Gerard Watson (Warminster, England: Aris and Phillips, 1990), p. 23.

†Ira Progoff provides careful guidance in this kind of work in *At a Journal Workshop*, pp. 127–40 and 267–85, and extends it to other key areas of life in describing dialogues with works, body, events, and society, pp. 123–94.

Working with SoulStirring Phrases

*See *The Well and the Cathedral* and *At a Journal Workshop*, pp. 312–49 and 392–96.

†See *Mantras for the Morning, Mantras for the Evening,* and *Mantras for the Midnight.*

Moving Beyond Words

*On the technique of clustering, see Tristine Rainer, *The New Diary,* chap. 9, and pp. 83–87 for the related technique of drawing maps of consciousness.

†Susanne Fincher provides a comprehensive guide to this kind of work in *Creating Mandalas for Insight, Healing, and Self-Expression.* See also Lucia Carpacione, *The Creative Journal.* On experiencing painting as a reflection of the soul, see Peter Rogers's *A Painter's Quest* and Sister Wendy Beckett's *The Gaze of Love.*

Clarifying Our Values and Beliefs

*For a more detailed description of how to do this work, see Progoff's *At a Journal Workshop,* pp. 310–11 and 350–58, and both volumes of George Simons's *Journal for Life.* See also Tristine Rainer's description of the technique of list-making in *The New Diary,* pp. 72–79.

†Examples of this kind of work abound. For some guidance in doing it, see Lois Daniel, *How to Write Your Own Life Story,* Sam Keen and Anne Valley-Fox's *Your Mythic Journey,* and Christian Hageseth III's *A Thirteen Moon Journal.*

Some Helpful Reading

The following books can help complement, enhance, expand, and enrich our personal practice of meditative writing through the diverse background, approaches, suggestions, exercises, and examples that they provide.

Adams, Kathleen. *Journal to the Self: Twenty-Two Paths to Personal Growth.* New York: Warner Books, 1990. The author presents this book as a "smorgasbord" of different techniques for journal writing as a therapeutic tool.

——. *The Way of the Journal: A Journal Therapy Workbook for Healing.* Lutherville, Md.: Sidran Press, 1993. Follows a "continuum of journal therapy" from structured or guided exercises to fluid and unstructured ones.

Baldwin, Christina. *One to One: Self-Understanding through Journal Writing.* New York: M. Evans & Co., 1977. A popular guidebook that provides exercises exemplifying the therapeutic value of journal writing as a pathway for self-understanding in eleven related areas of our lives.

——. *Life's Companion: Journal Writing as a Spiritual Quest.* New York: Bantam Books, 1991. An extensive work that combines personal reflections on the spiritual quest with corresponding journal exercises and quotations on the facing page.

Beckett, Sister Wendy. *The Gaze of Love: Meditations on Art and Spiritual Transformation.* New York: HarperCollins Publishers, 1993. Brief personal meditations on modern secular paintings that encourage the reader to see them as soul-stirring icons.

Cargas, Harry J., and Roger J. Radley. *Keeping a Spiritual Journal.* Garden City, New York: Doubleday and Co., 1981. A small book of questions and exercises designed to help young people get started in keeping a journal for personal and spiritual self-understanding; could also serve as a springboard for meditative writing for persons of any age.

Carpacione, Lucia. *The Creative Journal: The Art of Finding Yourself.* Athens, Ohio: Swallow Press, 1979. Outlines a personal process for journal writing with special emphasis on the importance of drawing and mandala work.

——. *The Well-Being Journal: Drawing on Your Inner Power to Heal Yourself.* Hollywood, Calif.: Newcastle Publishing, 1989. Presents journal writing and drawing as a pathway to personal healing and integrating body, mind, and spirit.

Daniel, Lois. *How to Write Your Own Life Story: A Step by Step Guide for the Non-Professional Writer.* Chicago: Chicago Review Press, 1985. A detailed guide for writing an autobiography for the family, and possibly for wider publication, that can be helpful in private autobiographical work as well.

D'Encarnacao, Paul S., and Patricia W. *The Joy of Journaling.* Memphis: Eagle Wing Books, 1991. A brief introduction to journal writing with exercises that include "soul work" and spirituality.

Dorff, O. Praem., Francis. "Intensive Journal Keeping: The Sound of Inner Music." *Emmanuel* (July–August, 1978), pp. 355-60. An introductory article that describes the integrating dynamics of Intensive Journal® writing through a musical metaphor of life's four voices.

——. "Spiritual Journal." *Westminster Dictionary of Christian Spirituality.* London: SCM Press, 1983. An historical overview of the character and importance of meditative writing in the Judeo-Christian tradition and in recent times.

——. "Meditative Writing." In Robert J. Wicks (ed.), *Handbook of Spirituality for Ministers.* New York: Paulist Press, 1995, pp. 153-73. The article on which this book is based.

Fincher, Susanne F. *Creating Mandalas for Insight, Healing, and Self-Expression.* Boston: Shambhala Books, 1991. A detailed, technical guide for creating and interpreting mandalas in terms of colors, numbers, forms, and developmental sequence.

Goldberg, Natalie. *Writing Down the Bones: Freeing the Writer Within.* Boston: Shambhala Books, 1986. Reflections and suggestions on how to write with the "essential, awake speech" of our minds.

Hageseth III, Christian. *A Thirteen Moon Journal: A Psychiatrist's Journey Toward Inner Peace.* Fort Collins, Colo.: Berwick Publishing, 1991. A book that introduces, describes, and exemplifies the advantages of writing a time-limited, private, edited "Portrait Journal" and suggests how to extend it by writing a public "Legacy Journal" for the family as a means of fostering interpersonal understanding.

Hinchman, Hannah. *A Life in Hand: Creating the Illuminated Journal.* Salt Lake City: Peregrine Smith Books, 1991. A book of exercises and examples that illustrates how writing, drawing, and calligraphy can be integrated in journaling.

Holzer, Burghild Nina. *A Walk Between Heaven and Earth: A Personal Journal on Writing and the Creative Process.* New York: Bell Tower, 1994. An engagingly written personal journal on the process of meditative writing that embodies and exemplifies the author's conviction that "the journal is a writing meditation, a walking meditation, a mystical journey."

Hughes, Mile. *Spiritual Journey Notebook.* Nashville: National Student Ministries, 1974. "A guide for personal spiritual growth through developing basic disciplines and specific actions in the Christian life."

Johnson, Robert A. *Inner Work: Using Dreams and Active Imagination for Personal Growth.* San Francisco: Harper and Row Inc., 1986. A thorough, practical guidebook to working with the unconscious dimension of our lives by applying a fourfold approach to working with dreams and active imagination.

Keen, Sam, and Anne Valley-Fox. *Your Mythic Journey: Finding Meaning in Your Life Through Writing and Storytelling.* Los Angeles: Jeremy P. Tarcher Inc., 1989. Evocative texts and writing exercises that invite the reader to explore life unfolding in past, present, future, and cosmic, or transpersonal, time.

Kelsey, Morton T. *Adventure Inward: Christian Growth Through Personal Journal Writing.* Minneapolis: Augsburg, 1980. A cogent presentation of the psychological and religious advantages of journal writing in the context of Christian faith. Includes dream work, suggested readings, and numerous examples from personal journals.

Klauser, Henriette Anne. *Writing On Both Sides of the Brain: Breakthrough Techniques for People Who Write.* San Francisco: Harper and Row Inc., 1987. Text and twenty exercises designed to help the reader break through writing anxieties and inhibitions by writing in a way that balances the intuitive and analytic sides of the brain.

Klug, Ronald. *How to Keep a Spiritual Journal: A Guide to Journal Keeping for Inner Growth and Personal Discovery.* Minneapolis: Augsburg Fortress Publishers, 1993. A holistic approach to journal writing in the context of Christian faith, emphasizing the personal benefits and practical techniques of journal writing.

Morneau, Robert F. *Mantras for the Morning: An Introduction to Holistic Prayer.* Collegeville, Minn.: The Liturgical Press, 1981. Twenty-five mantra meditations, including mantras, scriptural or poetic texts, photos, musical refrains, and prayerful reflections to exemplify and facilitate the practice of mantric prayer. The first in a trilogy of similarly designed books.

——. *Mantras for the Evening: The Experience of Holistic Prayer.* Collegeville, Minn.: The Liturgical Press, 1982.

——. *Mantras for the Midnight: Reflections for the Night Country.* Collegeville, Minn.: The Liturgical Press, 1985.

Nelson, G. Lynn. *Writing and Being: Taking Back Our Lives Through the Power of Language.* San Diego: Nelson, LuraMedia, 1994. A concise workbook presenting exercises in a process for relating private and public writing with personal growth.

Peace, Richard. *Spiritual Journaling: Recording Your Journey Toward God.* Colorado Springs, Colo.: Navpress, 1995. Drawing on the work of Ira Progoff, this book describes writing exercises for spiritually exploring and discussing the correlation between our personal stories and biblical stories within a group context. Includes schedule and guidelines for leading a group of this kind.

Pelikan, Jaroslav. "Writing as a Means of Grace." In Zinsser, William (ed.), *Spiritual Quests: The Art and Craft of Religious Writing.* Boston: Houghton Mifflin Co., 1988, pp. 83–101. A scholar's personal reflections on the spiritual importance of writing in the lives of Augustine, Newman, and Boethius.

Progoff, Ira. *At a Journal Workshop: Writing to Access the Power of the Unconscious and Evoke Creative Ability.* New York: Jeremy P. Tarcher Inc./Putnam, 1992. A one-volume condensation of two previous books (*At a Journal Workshop* and *The Practice of Process Meditation*) that serves as a self-contained workbook in Progoff's uniquely nonanalytic, intuitive, open-ended, and life-integrating approach to journal writing; presents an integrating sequence of exercises through which persons can explore the personal, therapeutic, creative, and spiritual value of journal writing. The text is complemented by an ongoing program of Intensive Journal® workshops designed by Dr. Progoff and sponsored by Dialogue House Associates, Inc., 80 East 11th Street, Suite 305, New York, N.Y. 10003, tel. (1-800) 221-5844.

——. *The Well and The Cathedral: An Entrance Meditation.* New York: Dialogue House, revised edition, 1983. The simplest, most direct introduction to the journal method of Ira Progoff. This book poetically describes a journey of meditative experience in a way that evokes meditative writing on the blank pages that face the text. Two other books in this entrance meditation series, namely *The White-Robed Monk* and *The Star/Cross,* as well as the cassette versions of all three books, are equally effective primers in meditative writing.

Rainer, Tristine. *The New Diary: How to Use a Journal for Self-Guidance and Expanded Creativity.* Los Angeles: Jeremy P. Tarcher Inc., 1978. A practical, detailed guidebook that draws on eight years of personal research and teaching in diary writing and on the pioneering work of Carl Jung, Ira Progoff, Marion Milner, and Anaïs Nin to present the New Diary movement as "an expanding new field of knowledge to be shared." Includes background, extensive exercises and examples, and an annotated bibliography.

Rico, Gabriele. *Pain and Possibility: Writing Your Way Through Personal Crisis.* Los Angeles: Jeremy P. Tarcher Inc., 1991. Highlights the therapeutic value of writing and clustering techniques as ways of naming, framing, and clarifying feelings and other personal inner experiences.

Rogers, Peter. *A Painter's Quest: Art as a Way of Revelation.* Santa Fe, N.M.: Bear and Company, 1988. A painter's meditative reflections on his paintings as expressions of his spiritual quest and on the creative process as it unfolded both consciously and unconsciously in his work. A remarkable contemporary example of icon meditation.

Santa-Maria, Maria L. *Growth through Meditation and Journal Writing: A Jungian Perspective on Christian Spirituality.* New York: Paulist Press, 1983. Draws on the Christian contemplative tradition, feminine consciousness, and Jungian psychology to present ways in which guided imagery and journaling can serve as tools for implementing a sevenfold program of "The Covenant Life" for adult Christian individuals and groups.

Schmidt, Joseph F. *Praying Our Experiences.* Winona, Minn.: Saint Mary's Press, 1984. An engaging essay by an experienced spiritual teacher on how writing can be a meditative way of rooting prayer in personal experience.

Simons, George F. *Journal for Life: Discovering Faith and Values through Journal Keeping, Part One: Foundation.* Chicago: ACTA, 1975. The first of two, small, practical workbooks focused on writing as a means of clarifying beliefs and values within the context of Christian faith; may easily be applied in other contexts.

———. *Journal for Life: Discovering Faith and Values through Journal Keeping, Part Two: Theology from Experience.* Chicago: ACTA, 1977.

———. *Keeping Your Personal Journal.* New York: Paulist Press, 1978. A simple, general introduction to resources and exercises in journal writing, including several exercises for "exploring soul country."

Snow, Kimberly, Ph.D. *Word Play/Word Power: A Woman's Personal Growth Workbook.* Berkeley, Calif.: Conari Press, 1989. Presents writing as a channel for women's personal growth through over seventy-five related readings and two hundred writing exercises.

Solly, Richard, and Roseann Lloyd. *Journey Notes: Writing for Recovery and Spiritual Growth.* San Francisco: Harper and Row Inc., 1989. Presents journal writing as a helpful tool in twelve-step recovery, and spiritual-growth work through a series of personal examples and over a hundred representative exercises.